W0254542

His Master's Words

His Master's Words

A Personal History of
Some Iconic Sikh Devotional Musicians
and Gurmat Sangeet

Harjap Singh Aujla

www.thebrowser.org
Publishers & Booksellers

Title – His Master's Words: A Personal History of
Some Iconic Sikh Devotional Musicians and Gurmat Sangeet
Author – Harjap Singh Aujla

ISBN – 978-93-92210-02-0
Edition – I

Published by –
J.G.S. Enterprises Pvt Ltd
Imprint – The Browser

Publisher's Address –
SCO 14-15, Sector 8-C, Chandigarh 160 009
Email: service@thebrowser.org.

Website – www.thebrowser.org
Email – service@the browser.org

Printed in India at Thomson Press (India) Ltd.

To my late parents:

Mr. Sochet Singh
and Mrs. Harjit Kaur

CONTENTS

Preface

My mother, Harjit Kaur, exposed me to *gurmat sangeet*[1] of the highest quality at a very young age and deserves full credit for inculcating the taste for Sikh religious music in me. When I was a little child, she taught me how to operate a radio receiver. A lot of credit also goes to the musicians of the Golden Temple of the bygone days, who consistently maintained a very high standard of music. I am talking of the early 1950s. Bhai Santa Singh was already the most respected *hazoori raagi*[2] of the Golden Temple and in 1947, Bhai Samund Singh joined him from the Gurdwara Janam Asthan Sri Nankana Sahib. Both were among the best musicians in their respective styles. My father, Sardar Sochet Singh, had purchased a complete set of twelve 78-RPM gramophone records of 'Asa Di Vaar'[3] rendered by Bhai

[1] The philosophy and tenets espoused by the Sikh Gurus, as enshrined in the Sri Guru Granth Sahib, is referred to as Gurmat. The music tradition based on this is known as Gurmat Sangeet.

[2] A raagi is a Sikh musician who plays hymns or shabads in different ragas as prescribed in the Sri Guru Granth Sahib. Hazoori means present, so the raagis deputed/appointed in the gurdwara for the daily recital of shabads is often referred to as the hazoori raagis.

[3] Rendition of 'Asa Di Vaar' is the real test of the merit of a Sikh religious musician. The earliest recordings of 'Asa Di Vaar' by Sikh musicians date back to the 1940s. These are by Budh Singh Taan of All India Radio Lahore on a set of 12 78-RPM records published by Young India Recording Company of Wadala in Bombay and a similar recording on a dozen 78-RPM records by Harbhajan Singh and Pradhan Singh published by the Gramophone Company of Calcutta India. It is also called His Master's Voice (HMV). During the 1960s two long playing records were released in the voice of Bhai Surjan Singh by the HMV, which became the best sellers. Bhai Piara Singh of the Golden Temple also had two

Budh Singh Taan published by the Young India Recording Company of Bombay. My mother encouraged me to play those records on a 1932-manufactured British-made HMV gramophone. This repeated practice made me a fan of Bhai Budh Singh Taan. These little gestures matter a lot to a child in his most impressionable years.

As I grew older, my curiosity and interest in Sikh music increased and I became a critic of Sikh religious music. I was fascinated by the art of our great musicians, and I tried to know the history of the greatest Sikh religious musicians of the yore. Of course, the Golden Temple is the oldest source of gurmat sangeet for musicians as it has been performed there regularly for more than 400 years. This temple has been a witness to the changing trends in Sikh music since the days of dominance of *dhrupad, dhamar* and *partals*[4].

The other leading centre of music has been the Gurdwara Janam Asthan Sri Nankana Sahib, which now falls in Pakistan. This gurdwara was developed primarily during the reign of Emperor Ranjit Singh and his father. When this gurdwara was established, the north Indian classical music had undergone a change from the dhrupad and dhamar style to *khayal, thumri, dadra, tappa, hori*[5] etc. I

---

popular long-playing records of 'Asa Di Vaar', but the recording of 'Asa Di Vaar' by Bhai Nirmal Singh broke all previous records, and 6.5 million copies were sold throughout the world! Famous *raagis* of the older times used to say that the real test of the brilliance of a Sikh religious musician lies in his professionalism in rendition of the 'Asa Di Vaar'. Bhai Nirmal Singh Khalsa has established his credentials most admirably.

[4] Taal in Indian classical music refers to the musical meter, i.e., the rhythmic beat that measures musical time. It complements the raaga which is the melodic framework for improvisation and composition. Dhrupad is a genre in Hindustani classical music and its oldest known style. Dhamar is one of the taals associated with the dhrupad style and typically played on the pakhawaj and also tabla. In a partal the same shabad is rendered in several taals for the asthai (the initial phrase of a melodic composition) and antras (the equivalent of a verse). It is the gift of the great Gurus.

[5] Semi-classical forms of Indian music.

have tried to compare the styles of gurmat sangeet at these leading centres of Sikh music.

After 1947, Nankana Sahib was ethnically cleansed of its entire Sikh population and overnight it ceased to remain a centre of Sikh religious music. Its place was taken by the historic gurdwaras of Delhi. Boasting of the largest Sikh population in any urban area of India, due to mass resettlement of Sikh refugees from Pakistan, Delhi developed into an emerging competitor for the Golden Temple. As of this moment, thanks to the faulty recruitment policy at the Golden Temple, the historic gurdwaras of Delhi are forging ahead of the Golden Temple.

I have tried to study the lives of the leading exponents of gurmat sangeet in East Punjab, Pakistan, and Delhi. The first life sketch that I have written about a *kirtania*[6] pertains to Bhai Jwala Singh, who was born in 1872 and died in 1952. The second one is about Bhai Samund Singh, born in 1900 and died in 1972. The third includes the life story of Bhai Santa Singh, born in 1904 (some historians think it is 1912) and who died in 1966.

The other chapters include one on Bhai Jwala Singh's sons, Bhai Avtar Singh and Bhai Gurcharan Singh, and another on his grandson, Bhai Kultar Singh, originally of Sultanpur Lodhi. There are write-ups on Bhai Gurmukh Singh, Sarmukh Singh Fakkar of Sri Nankana Sahib, Bhai Pal Singh Bhai Jaswant Singh and their second generation of Sri Nankana Sahib. Some of the other chapters include information on Bhai Joginder Singh and Mohinder Singh also of Sri Nankana Sahib, Bhai Piara Singh, Bhai Harjinder Singh of Srinagar, and Bhai Dilbagh Singh Gulbagh Singh of Jalandhar.

Some others about whom I have written include Bhai Bakhshish Singh, Bhai Balbir Singh, Bhai Nirmal Singh

---

[6] One who performs kirtan, another name for raagi.

Khalsa, and Bhai Gurmeet Singh Shant, all of whom, at one time or the other, were associated with the Golden Temple. Some freelance kirtanias find mention too. They include Bhai Dharam Singh Zakhmi, Bhai Didar Singh of Nangal Khurd district Hoshiarpur, Dr Jagir Singh of Chandigarh, and his youngest brother, Dr Gurnam Singh of Patiala.

There are some other brilliant kirtanias of the Golden Temple like Bhai Sunder, Bhai Moti, Bhai Hira Singh, Bhai Faiz, Bhai Lal, Bhai Chand, Bhai Chhaila, Bhai Desa, Bhai Taba, Bhai Rashida, Bhai Bilasa, Bhai Gam and some others about whom I did not write due to lack of knowledge or unauthenticated information. Also, due to lack of information, I did not write about some others like Bhai Gian Singh Almast and his son, Thakar Singh, Bhai Beant Singh Bijli, Bhai Davinder Singh of Gurdaspur, Bhai Gian Singh Surjeet, Bhai Partap Singh, Bhai Surjan Singh, Bhai Gopal Singh, Bhai Harbans Singh of Jagadhri, Bhai Hari Singh and many others. I regret these omissions.

I have written this book with esteem for all and malice towards none of the kirtanias. To the best of my knowledge, no book has been written on this subject in English, although a lot of material exists in Punjabi. I hope that readers will like this humble attempt.

Harjap Singh Aujla
e-mail address: harjapaujla@gmail.com
Phone Number + 91 98149 06024
April 2022

1

Contrasting Styles of Gurmat Sangeet

The Golden Temple and Nankana Sahib

Gurdwara Sri Darbar Sahib or Sri Harimandir Sahib (now popularly known as the Golden Temple) in Amritsar has been a centre of gurmat sangeet since its inception more than 400 years ago. This is the place, where legendry Sikh religious musicians gave their best from time to time. They were the finest *dhrupadias, dhamarias* and *partalias*[7].

The holy Sri Guru Granth Sahib *ji* was compiled only a short distance away from Sri Darbar Sahib. The gurbani (in poetical form) of the first five Gurus, along with similar teachings of several other religious preachers, were entered into the holy book by prescribing its recitation into 31 distinct raagas. The fifth Guru, Sri Guru Arjan Dev ji, got it written by Bhai Gurdas ji in his own handwriting, and after its completion, the Sri Guru Granth Sahib ji was formally installed in the sanctum sanctorum of the Darbar Sahib. From then on recitation of the hymns from the Sri Guru Granth Sahib ji started in this highly revered shrine.

[7] Singers of dhrupad, dhamar and partal.

Famous traditional musicians hailing from the *rababi*[8] community to which Bhai Mardana belonged, like Bhai Satta, Bhai Balwand, and others used to sing gurbani in Sri Darbar Sahib during Guru Arjan Dev ji's lifetime.

Most of the time, the first Guru, Sri Guru Nanak Dev ji, gave his sermons and discourses in the local language in poetical format. During his numerous travels of Hindustan and abroad, he was accompanied by a Muslim rababi musician, Bhai Mardana, who provided the instrumental accompaniment on all his *udasis*[9] of the then known world, whenever Guru Nanak Dev ji did a rendition of his gurbani. Every time that Guru Nanak Dev ji ventured out, Bhai Mardana was at his beck and call with his rabab. This instrument is prevalent even to this day in Afghanistan, the Northwest Frontier area of Pakistan, and Kashmir. The rabab was also capable of creating the beat; therefore, the presently-used drums were not considered necessary in Guru Nanak Dev ji's time. However, during the time of the later Gurus, drums like the tabla, dholaki and pakhawaj were commonly used in Sikh religious music. The dhadd[10] came to be used during the time of the sixth Guru.

Dhrupad and khayal are two distinctly independent streams of classical music. The dhrupad and dhamar styles of classical music are taal (beat) centric and are now dying all over India including Punjab. Dhrupad is the oldest known form of rendition of North Indian classical music. This form of music was prevalent during the times of the ten Gurus of the Sikh faith. Some scholars are of the opinion that this style of classical singing was evolved by the pandits (Hindus

---

[8] Rababis are descendants of Bhai Mardana, who accompanied Guru Nanak on the latter's far-flung travels with a musical instrument called the rabab.

[9] Tours of Guru Nanak

[10] The dhadd is made of wood with thin a waist like an hourglass. The skin on both sides is tightened with ropes that help in holding the instrument firmly together. Its design is very similar to other Indian drums.

of the Brahmin upper-caste descent, who used to be the scholars of old Sanskrit language and classical musicians) thousands of years ago and they kept evolving and sophisticating their music over the medieval centuries. However, as far as Sikh music is concerned, there is no denying the fact that during the lifetime of the founder of the faith, Sri Guru Nanak Dev ji, the dhrupad *shaili*[11] of classical music was alive and flourishing all over the Indo-Gangetic heartland. The great masters like Tansen and Baiju Bawara were both exponents of the dhrupad shaili form of music. Even the legendry Hazrat Amir Khusro had undergone training in the dhrupad format of classical music. Guru Nanak Dev ji was by no means alien to this sophisticated form of classical music either.

On the other hand, khayal *gayaki*[12], which is very popular in northern India these days, was going through a process of evolution during the time of the tenth Guru, Gobind Singh ji (1666 to 1708). He evolved a form of *tarana*[13] singing in his court. The semi-classical formats like dadra, thumri, tappa and *kajri* were later innovations. Khayal gayaki was known to Guru Gobind Singh ji and he composed his own khayals too. He wrote his *baani*[14] in several meters, untried by his predecessors. Due to his strict adherence to the meters, it is easy to sing his baanis. The khayal stream of music is flourishing in virtually every *gharana*[15] of India, including the Patiala gharana.

---

[11] Style or form.

[12] Singing style.

[13] Tarana is a type of composition in Hindustani classical vocal music in which certain words and languages based on Persian and Arabic phonemes are rendered at a medium (madhya laya) or fast (drut laya) pace. It was invented by Amir Khusro.

[14] A term used by Sikhs to refer to various sections of the Holy Text that appears in their several Holy Books like the Sri Guru Granth Sahib.

[15] It typically refers to the place where the musical ideology originated.

Dhrupad has a distinct taal for drummers and the singing revolves around this. In khayal gayaki the singer has the liberty to choose any one of the taals for the slow tempo of the music and switch over to other taals for the medium and fast tempo of the music. This makes khayal singing full of several permutations and combinations of taals.

Sikh historians are unanimous in their belief that Guru Nanak Dev ji was a great musician. His instrumentalist companion, Bhai Mardana, was also from a caste of traditional musicians. The succeeding Gurus also composed the gurbani in poetical rhythms and was prescribed to be rendered in certain raagas.

From the time of the fifth master, music has been a regular feature in Gurdwara Sri Darbar Sahib in Amritsar. Most of the early musicians there were from the rababi caste of Muslim musicians. This community learnt the ancient art of gurmat sangeet from one generation to the other. So, the *reets*[16] were kept alive within the closely-knit families.

In earlier times, Sikhs of the Gurus were not so good at gurmat sangeet. Therefore, most of the time-specific *chowkis*[17] of gurmat sangeet at the Darbar Sahib in Amritsar were rendered by rababi Muslim musicians only. The only notable exception was Bhai Mansha Singh, a highly dedicated *gursikh*[18] kirtania during the reign of Emperor Ranjit Singh. The practising Sikhs, barring a few families, took over in the twentieth century, mostly after 1947, when the Shiromani Gurdwara Prabandhak Committee[19] (SGPC) banned non-Sikhs from kirtan.

---

[16] Traditions.

[17] Session or conclave.

[18] A Sikh who is especially devoted to following the Sikh guru, a "pious, observant Sikh".

[19] An organization responsible for the management of gurdwaras in the three states of Punjab, Haryana, and Himachal Pradesh and union territory of Chandigarh. SGPC also administers Darbar Sahib in Amritsar.

There were times when the sixth Guru, Hargobind Sahib, fought four battles against the ruling Mughal soldiers. Chowkis of shabad kirtan were temporarily interrupted during these battles. Also, during the time of the plundering and massacring invasions of India by Nadir Shah during 1739 and Ahmed Shah Abdali from 1748 to 1767, there were regular interruptions in shabad kirtan at the Sri Darbar Sahib. These were harrowing times when the practising Sikhs were hounded by the Islamic rulers of Lahore and Amritsar, and the time-sensitive gurmat sangeet chowkis during this time were badly inhibited.

Several state-authorised attempts were made to destroy the Sri Darbar Sahib itself between 1739 and 1767! However, every time it was damaged or desecrated, it was quickly rebuilt by the Guru's devout Sikhs.

During these difficult times, the rababi Muslim musicians of Amritsar and its surroundings also went into hiding. Sikh religious music was, however, kept alive by them within the four walls of their homes. They used to teach music and gurbani behind closed doors from father to son and from son to grandson. This fact was told to my father by a rababi kirtania and an accomplished drummer, Bhai Chanan of Kapurthala, prior to his forced migration to Pakistan during the communal disturbances of 1947. He belonged to the Goindwal Sahib ancestry.

There was a huge catchment area of musicians serving at the Sri Darbar Sahib that comprised Khadoor Sahib, Tarn Taran Sahib, Goindwal Sahib, Sultanpur Lodhi, and Kapurthala. To begin with, all these musicians were accomplished dhrupadias and dhamarias. The beats they used included not just the dadra, *teen* taal and the *kehrwa,* but uncommon ones too like the *deep chandi, jhap taal, chhotti teen taal, roopak taal, yakka, chaar taal, and the panj taal,* to name a few. Most of the musicians had years of training and practice before they qualified as musicians of the Sri Darbar Sahib. After all, the Gurus had laid stringent standards for the rendition of gurmat sangeet, and only those who could adhere to these lofty traditions were given duties to perform music at Sri Darbar Sahib.

When Shukarchakia Sikh Misl[20], led by Sardar Charhat Singh and Maha Singh, took over the control of Gujranwala in the second half of the eighteenth century, some religious activity started in the Nankana Sahib area. The place where Sri Guru Nanak Dev ji was born was known to every knowledgeable inhabitant as Rai Bhoin Di Talwandi, but the proper gurdwara known as Gurdwara Janam Asthan Sri Nankana Sahib took form only during the reign of Emperor Ranjit Singh. As the building came up at the birthplace of Sri Guru Nanak Dev ji, musicians and *granthis*[21] were also recruited. This happened approximately 200 years ago in the early 1820s. Most able-bodied practising Sikhs were recruited into the army of Emperor Ranjit Singh and the duty of performing gurmat sangeet at Gurdwara Janam Asthan once again fell on the shoulders of the rababi Muslim musicians. Most of these musicians living around Nankana Sahib were obviously the first to be recruited. They were followed by musicians from Lahore, Gujranwala, and Gujarat areas. Some arrived from different parts of Amritsar too.

By the time Emperor Ranjit Singh conquered most of central Punjab and annexed Lahore and Amritsar, obviously, some musicians from these regions also became musicians at Gurdwara Janam Asthan. Thus, there came up another

---

[20] The misls were the twelve sovereign states of the Sikh Confederacy, which rose during the 18th century in the Punjab region in the northern part of the Indian subcontinent and is cited as one of the causes of the weakening of the Mughal Empire prior to Nader Shah's invasion of India in 1738–1740. The Shukarchakia misl is the one to which Emperor Ranjit Singh belonged.

[21] Priests who act as custodians of the Sri Guru Granth Sahib, the sacred scripture of the Sikhs.

parallel centre of music. By this time, khayal gayaki had become the popular format of classical music. The changes in music that took place in Benares, Lucknow, Allahabad, Agra, Gwalior, and Delhi travelled as far away as Lahore in Punjab as well. Both Amritsar and Nankana Sahib also came under the influence of Lahore's musical innovations. Since the dhrupad and dhamar styles of music were already well-entrenched at the Sri Darbar Sahib in Amritsar, the transition to khayal gayaki was not smooth, at least in Amritsar. Some reets were in vogue during the times of the ten Gurus. These reets retained their prominent position up to the middle of the twentieth century. The great Gurus also used regional folk music like *chhants, ghorian and alahunians* in their renditions. Unfortunately, due to the rapidly falling standard of hazoori raagis at the Sri Darbar Sahib, these folk tunes are also on the verge of extinction even in Amritsar.

I know about a family of practising Sikhs who were originally living in Fateabad near Tarn Taran (formerly in Amritsar district). This is the ancestral place from where the brave Sikh general, Nawab Jassa Singh Ahluwala, hailed. Later, this family of musicians moved to the small hamlet of Saidpur near Sultanpur Lodhi in the princely state of Kapurthala. Their traditional style of music was based on dhrupad and dhamar varieties. The most famous musician of this family was the late Bhai Jwala Singh (1872–1952). He was trained by his father, Bhai Dewa Singh, who was also a leading kirtania, and another highly accomplished trainer, Bhai Rangi Ram, originally of Tarn Taran area, but later settled in Amritsar. According to Bhai Jwala Singh's sons, Bhai Avtar Singh and Bhai Gurcharan Singh, their illustrious father knew approximately 500 reets for the recitation of gurbani that were derived from the 31 raagas mentioned in the Sri Guru Granth Sahib ji. It is claimed by this duo that all these 500 reets used to be sung at the Sri

Darbar Sahib at one time or the other during the past 400 years or so. Bhai Jwala Singh was adept in the partal format of classical singing too. This is a variant off-shoot from the dhrupad and dhamar style of music. In partal, a number of taals are used for the same shabad for the rendition of various *shlokas*[22]. Even partal is a dying art now.

Since Bhai Jwala Singh lived in village Saidpur and performed shabad kirtan in Sultanpur Lodhi and nearby Kapurthala, far away from the ever-changing music and culture of Lahore and Delhi, the khayali style of Hindustani classical music did not impact his centuries-old original musical style. Therefore, his style of music maintained its purity. Prior to his demise in 1952, Bhai Jwala Singh taught all his reets to his sons. His son, Bhai Gurcharan Singh, taught all the taals for playing the tabla to his nephew, Bhai Swaran Singh. Roughly from 1946 to 1951, Bhai Swaran Singh accompanied Bhai Jwala Singh on the tabla. In 1952, the former stopped kirtan due to age-related problems, and Swaran Singh was asked to join the group of Bhai Avtar Singh and Gurcharan Singh.

The newly formed trio of musicians started independently performing shabad kirtan in 1952 at Sultanpur Lodhi, Kapurthala, and Jalandhar. They also became radio artists at All India Radio Jalandhar-Amritsar. Later, they moved to Delhi and performed shabad kirtan at the Gurdwara Sri Sisganj Sahib in Old Delhi, Gurdwara Bangla Sahib, Gurdwara Mata Sundari, and Gurdwara Raqab Ganj Sahib in New Delhi. As long as Bhai Avtar Singh and Gurcharan Singh were alive, they maintained the purity of their style of music. Now Bhai Avtar Singh's son, Bhai Kultar Singh, who is an engineer by profession, leads the *kirtani jatha*[23] and even he has retained purity in the reets.

---

[22] A poetic form used in Sanskrit.

[23] A group of raagis (usually three) doing kirtan together.

Bhai Kultar Singh has a very sweet voice and his range of producing the lower and higher notes is commendable.

Bhai Baldeep Singh is another prominent scholar of gurmat sangeet within the extended Saidpur family. He is a good musical instrument maker too. He has made the saranda, taus and the rabab. He has tuned and tested these instruments and found them worthy of use. Theoretically, his knowledge of music is very good, but for singing purposes, he requires a lot more *riyaz*[24]. He has quite good a command of English and Italian languages, which serve him in good stead in interfaith dialogues.

I have tried to compare Bhai Avtar Singh and Bhai Gurcharan Singh's style of performing shabad kirtan with that of Bhai Santa Singh (1904–1966). Due to his high-pitched voice, he initially encountered resistance from the other kirtanias of the Golden Temple, but ultimately, his merit prevailed and he was accepted as a worthy musician. From 1925–1949 he served at the Golden Temple in Amritsar as one of the leading kirtanias. For a male singer his shrill voice was initially a liability, but eventually became his asset as he could effortlessly sing in very high and low notes. In 1949, he first moved to Assam for doing some contract work with the Government, where he did not succeed, and then finally, he moved to Delhi to become the most respected kirtania of the National Capital Region. I can find lots of similarities in their styles of rendition. Their pattern of rendition of 'Asa Di Vaar' is also very similar.

Bhai Santa Singh's nephews, Bhai Harjit Singh and Bhai Gurdip Singh, also are the leading kirtanias of New Delhi. They sing all the reets of Bhai Santa Singh and their kirtan style also resembles that of Bhai Avtar Singh and Gurcharan Singh. Now their successor is Bhai Kultar Singh. I have also found some similarities in the kirtan style of Bhai Balbir

---

[24] Practice.

Singh of the Golden Temple and Bhai Avtar Singh Gurcharan Singh. All this goes to prove that the age-old traditions of performing shabad kirtan at the Golden Temple based on the dhrupad and dhamar styles of classical music had been evolved by the great Gurus. Guru Nanak Dev ji is credited with evolving raaga Asa and perhaps Sri raaga too. Some raagis sing Babe Nanak Di Basant as well.

The rababi kirtanias of the Golden Temple, like Bhai Lal Senior (a descendent of Bhai Abdullah and Bhai Nath Mal of the period of Sri Guru Teg Bahadur Sahib ji), Bhai Chand, Bhai Gam, Bhai Faiz, Bhai Desa, Bhai Taba, Bhai Sunder, Bhai Moti and Bhai Nasira (a descendent of Bhai Satta and Bhai Balwand of the time of the fourth Guru, Sri Guru Ram Das ji and the fifth Guru, Sri Guru Arjan Dev ji), all had their own characteristics of performing shabad kirtan and each one differed from the others in style and riyaz. All of them, though, had great riyaz behind their singing styles.

I must admit that all the rababis were quite adept in *taan paltas*[25]. Bhai Sain Ditta rababi was an accomplished tutor of rendition of gurbani in ancient traditions. He was the head tutor at Amritsar's famous Yateemkhana. Among his *shagirds*[26] were Bhai Santa Singh, Bhai Dharam Singh Zakhmi, and Bhai Darshan Singh Komal to name a few. Bhai Darshan Singh Komal became a great trainer in his own right and his finest student was a blind kirtania, the late Bhai Didar Singh of village Nangal Khurd in Hoshiarpur district. The others included Bhai Beant Singh Bijli of Phillaur and Bhai Gian Singh Surjeet of the United Kingdom.

I have also had the experience of listening to the gurmat sangeet of the most prominent musicians of Sri Nankana Sahib, the late Bhai Samund Singh, who served Gurdwara Janam Asthan for 35 years from 1912 to 1947. He was born

---

[25] Reversing the taan.

[26] Disciples.

in 1900, and due to his intensive training in gurmat sangeet at a very young age, as well as his remembering by the heart of a significant number of shabads written in the holy Sri Guru Granth Sahib, he was approved as a hazoori raagi of Gurdwara Janam Asthan at the young age of 12 years. Due to his long hours of riyaz every day, he had great command over gurmat sangeet. What I found unique in his style was that he excelled in the rendition of *chhotta* raaga, which in other words means singing in just the *madh lai*[27]. He generally avoided singing of complete khayal, which started from *alaap,* then went to *jorh alaap,*[28] *vilambit lai,*[29] madh lai and finally climax in the *dhrutt lai*. This is the proper way of khayal singing. Bhai Samund Singh attached great importance to the prominence of gurbani rendition, making it clear that the raaga does not diminish the importance of the Guru's word. In some of his renditions, he used the thumri style of singing. I have observed even the style of Multani Qafi in his singing. Ustad Bade Ghulam Ali Khan, the most prominent exponent of the Patiala Gharana of North Indian classical music and his younger brother, Barqat Ali Khan, were Bhai Samund Singh's radio singer contemporaries and best friends. They learnt a lot from one another, and they admired one another's styles as well.

I also heard the gurmat sangeet of some of the other musicians who migrated from Nankana Sahib to India and their second generation, who were also born in Nankana Sahib, but gained adulthood in India. To start with they were all Muslim rababis, but at the height of the Singh Sabha[30] movement in Punjab, during the first two decades of

---

[27] *Madh lai:* Medium tempo.

[28] *Jorh alaap*: Alaap including drumbeat.

[29] *Vilambat lai*: Slow Tempo.

[30] A Sikh movement that began in Punjab in the 1870s in reaction to the proselytising activities of Christians, Hindu reform movements (Brahmo Samajis, Arya Samaj) and Muslims (Aligarh movement and Ahmadiyah). It culminated in

the twentieth century, several of their ancestors became *amritdhari*[31] Sikhs. Some of the musicians of the first generation, about whom I have heard, were Bhai Pal Singh and Jaswant Singh. Their second-generation included Bhai Prithipal, Bhai Mohan Pal Singh, and Bhai Kishan Pal Singh. Both Bhai Prithipal Singh and Bhai Mohan Pal Singh learnt every detail of music from Bhai Pal Singh. I particularly liked the rich male voice of Bhai Mohan Pal Singh. His riyaz of the raagas was amazing. His admirers were far fewer in India than abroad. Most of his finest recordings were also made abroad. Bhai Mohan Pal Singh was a complete khayal singer and so was Bhai Prithipal Singh. They would perform alaap for several minutes and then move to vilambit lai, then to dhrutt lai as the climax. I firmly believe that during the time of the great Gurus, there was no such thing as the dhrutt lai. I also feel that the dhrupad and dhamar styles suit gurmat sangeet a lot more than the khayali format of music. Thumri, which is sung in one lai more suited to gurbani *gayan*, as are dadra and *multani* and Sindhi *kafi*.

Another great raagi jatha from Gurdwara Janam Asthan Sri Nankana Sahib consisted of the two brothers, Bhai Gurmukh Singh and Bhai Sarmukh Singh Fakkar. Bhai Gurmukh Singh had no children, but his brother, Sarmukh Singh's son, Bhai Jagtar Singh, carried forward their musical traditions. I had no chance of listening to Bhai Gurmukh Singh and Sarmukh Singh Fakkar, but Bhai Jagtar Singh Fakkar emphatically claimed that he was the true exponent of their style of shabad kirtan. A couple of gramophone records of shabad kirtan were published in their voices. I have no reason to disbelieve what Bhai Jagtar Singh claims. Also, I have several of his recordings and I say with certainty

the creation of the SGPC.

[31] *Amritdhari* Sikhs are practicing Sikhs with unshorn hair and the five *kakars*.

that he was by himself a highly accomplished kirtania.

The styles of shabad kirtan of Bhai Pal Singh and Bhai Jaswant Singh as well as Bhai Gurmukh Singh and Sarmukh Singh Fakkar are more or less identical. This I can claim from the recordings of Bhai Prithipal Singh and Bhai Mohan Pal Singh as well as of Bhai Jagtar Singh Fakkar and his sons.

There is another branch of second-generation rababi kirtanias of Nankana Sahib known as Bhai Joginder Singh and Bhai Mohinder Singh. For several years, they were hazoori raagis at the Dukhniwaran Sahib Gurdwara in Patiala and the Takhat Sri Huzoor Sahib at Nanded in Maharashtra. Even their style is not much different from the other two branches. All of them perform kirtan in typical khayal gayaki, which is quite different from the traditional gurmat sangeet that is performed at the Golden Temple and the other historic shrines in its catchment area like the gurdwaras at Khadoor Sahib, Tarn Taran Sahib, Sultanpur Lodhi, and Kapurthala.

Bhai Jagtar Singh Fakkar's elder sons, Bhai Harcharan Singh and Bhai Harinder Singh Fakkar were also highly accomplished kirtanias with very melodious voices. They were the third generation of kirtanias of Gurdwara Janam Asthan Sri Nankana Sahib. Both of them are now no more. It has been observed that the rababi kirtanias don't cross the sixties in age! Why I don't know.

Now Bhai Harcharan Singh Fakkar's son, Bhai Lal Singh Fakkar, is also leading a raagi jatha. Bhai Dalip Singh, another son of Bhai Jagtar Singh Fakkar, is also a kirtania. They are keeping their ancestral style of shabad kirtan alive long after their forced migration to India in 1947. It is an irony that none of them stayed back in Nankana Sahib.

In August 1947, the Sikhs living in Nankana Sahib did not want to leave the birthplace of Sri Guru Nanak Dev ji. They were deeply attached to the birthplace of the founder of their religion. Several attempts were made to dislodge them, but each time they fought back fiercely. Eventually, Baloch soldiers, supported by artillery, were deployed to dislodge them. When they finally left after bloody exchanges of fierce street battles, not even one Sikh was left to take care of the holy Sri Guru Granth Sahib. This situation stayed for a long time after 1947. Both Bhai Mohan Pal Singh and Bhai Jagtar Singh had identical stories to tell. In fact, ever since 1947, Gurdwara Janam Asthan has ceased to be a centre of gurmat sangeet. Pakistan realised her folly of total ethnic cleansing of the Sikh community only years later.

I can conclude with confidence that since Gurdwara Janam Asthan was established less than 250 years ago, its musical traditions are not as old as those of the Golden Temple, which is far more like the music of the times of the first five Gurus. I have also seen that there is a marked difference in the styles of shabad kirtan of the rababi musicians of the Golden Temple and the new-age Sikhs. The former have more mastery over the raagas and their voices are more cultured while the latter know more of Gurbani and they don't let raagas dominate Gurbani. Some of the rababis, after becoming practising Sikhs for more than one generation, have changed their style, laying more stress on the recitation of Gurbani than on taan paltas. Bhai Dharam Singh Zakhmi was one of the rababi kirtanias who became a leading interpreter of the Guru's word.

I know of one more family of Sikh religious musicians, who hailed from the Gujrat district in Pakistani Punjab. After migrating to East Punjab, they settled in Fatehgarh Sahib (Sirhind) in Patiala. Their father, Bhai Uttam Singh Patang, was a reputed kirtania in his own right. He became one of the hazoori raagis of Gurdwara Fatehgarh Sahib. His elder son, Dr Jagir Singh, did a PhD in gurmat sangeet and became a very profound kirtania. His voice is sweet like honey. For some time, he accompanied Bhai Bakhshish Singh of the Golden Temple as a part of his raagi jatha and learnt a lot from the great master. His second son, Dr Bachittar Singh, also did a PhD and is a good Sikh religious musician. His third son, Dr Gurnam Singh, first tried his hand at *ghazal*[32] singing and became a radio singer at All India Radio, Jalandhar. Later, he did his PhD in music and became a professor in the musicology department of Punjabi University in Patiala and retired from there as the head of the Department of Sikh Musicology. He maintained a regular regime of riyaz while performing his teaching duties. He retired recently. Dr Gurnam Singh is credited for building the great library of gurmat sangeet at the Punjabi University in Patiala.

Today the Punjabi University has a huge library of rare recordings of gurmat sangeet. This unique project was initiated by the highly motivated professor, Dr Taran Singh, under whose guidance a lot of rare recordings in the voices of legendry Bhai Samund Singh and Bhai Avtar Singh Gurcharan Singh were made and stored. Having access to rare recordings helped Dr Gurnam Singh immensely. He studied the rare, recorded music with great curiosity and also kept doing riyaz of what he learnt. He listened to some reets repeatedly. Due to his perseverance, he kept rising in his stature in the university and ultimately rose to the highest position. Now after retirement, he visits the USA and Canada quite often.

Today Dr Gurnam Singh has evolved his own distinct style of performing gurmat sangeet by amalgamating all that he has learnt. He is in great demand in the USA for teaching music to budding musicians. His style of music is neither of

---

[32] The ghazal is a form of amatory poem or ode, originating in Arabic poetry, as an expression of both the pain of loss or separation and the beauty of love in spite of that pain.

the Golden Temple nor of the Gurdwara Janam Asthan. It is something in between the various styles. He often visits India and performs shabad kirtan at different gurdwaras. In America, there is a huge demand for learning Sikh religious music, and Dr Gurnam Singh is filling that vacuum.

Coming back to the Golden Temple, the standard of music here was very high in the first half of the twentieth century when the line-up of gurmat musicians consisted of the practising Sikhs as well as the rababi Muslims. We had musicians like Bhai Moti, Bhai Sunder, Bhai Agha Faiz, Bhai Hira Singh, Bhai Bhag Singh, Bhai Gam, Bhai Lal, Bhai Chand, Bhai Desa, Bhai Taba, Bhai Bilasa, Bhai Santa Singh, Bhai Samund Singh, Bhai Santokh Singh, Bhai Balbir Singh and the like. After a protracted struggle for freedom, India attained independence, but it was unfortunately associated with the division of the Punjab province. Most of the rababi Muslim musicians were forced out of East Punjab to settle down in West Punjab (Pakistan). West Punjab was ethnically cleansed of almost all the Sikhs.

Bhai Chand, a leading Muslim musician of the Golden Temple, who could not adjust to the circumstances leading to his reduced status in Pakistan, eventually committed suicide. First, he was humiliated by the post-1947 narrowness generated in the Indian-Sikh community to leave Amritsar and then he was equally disrespected in Pakistan when there was no demand for his music in that country. There was a time when his finances had dwindled so low that he had to sleep on the floor on an empty stomach! The Pakistan Government had refused to give him even the minimum pension owing to his old age and poor finances. He even tried selling fruit as a squatter, but that did not work either. In utter frustration, one day he committed suicide.

The momentum of the pre-1947 years of excellence in music continued for a few years, but from the 1960s, the standard of musicians has been falling continuously at the Golden Temple. In sharp comparison, the musicians in Delhi have consistently maintained a high standard of music. The torchbearer of good Sikh music in Delhi has been Bhai Santa Singh, formerly of the Golden Temple. The others were Bhai Avtar Singh, Gurcharan Singh, Swaran Singh, Bhai Shamsher Singh, Jabarjang Singh, Bhai Takhat Singh, Bhai Mangal Singh, Bhai Shamsher Singh Zakhmi, Bhai Harjit Singh, Gurdeep Singh, and Bhai Manohar Singh, just to name a few.

Bhai Harjit Singh Gurdeep Singh

Of late, at the Golden Temple, the selection process of musicians has come into the hands of those who neither have any knowledge of the raagas nor any command over gurbani and its appropriate pronunciation. Some accomplished musicians found due respect as the hazoori musicians even through the faulty selection process. These worthy musicians, who were made to struggle included Bhai Balbir Singh, Bhai Hari Singh, Bhai Amrik Singh, Bhai Kirpal Singh, Bhai Gurmej Singh, Bhai Bakhshish Singh, Bhai Piara Singh, Bhai Chattar Singh Sindhi, Bhai Narinder Singh Benarasi, Bhai Nirmal Singh Khalsa, Bhai Randhir Singh, Bhai Gurmeet Singh Shant, Bhai Harjinder Singh Srinagarwale, Bhai Sarabjit Singh Laddi, Bhai Gurmel Singh, and Bhai Rai Singh. Some were rehabilitated before death, some others died struggling for respect. Some are alive.

Some worthy musicians from Delhi, Patna Sahib, and Huzoor Sahib also occasionally get chances to perform shabad kirtan at the Golden Temple. I remember, whenever Bhai Avtar Singh and Bhai Gurcharan Singh visited the Golden Temple, they recited gurbani kirtan in the sanctum sanctorum. Similarly, Bhai Sarbjeet Singh Rangeela of Durgh near Raipur in Chhattisgarh was invited to perform gurmat sangeet at the Golden Temple. Bhai Joginder Singh and Mohinder Singh of Takhat Sri Huzoor Sahib were also accorded this privilege during their visits to Amritsar. Bhai Taba rababi, on his numerous visits to India, after the creation of Pakistan, was consulted on the intricacies of gurmat sangeet by some of the highly respected musicians like Bhai Santa Singh. The non-practising Sikhs, though, are still not allowed to perform kirtan at the historic shrines.

After the creation of Pakistan in August 1947, there was a time when there was no one in Pakistan who could continue the daily duties at the important Sikh shrines. These included recitation of hymns from the Guru Granth Sahib and daily *ardas*[33] at the Gurdwara Janam Asthan. Within a few years of 1947, the animosity between the Muslims and the Sikhs had subsided. At this time, Pakistan decided to restore some limited services at Gurdwara Janam Asthan, Gurdwara Dera Sahib at Lahore and Gurdwara Panja Sahib at Hassan Abdal. The Government of Pakistan also showed keenness to allow some Sikhs from India to visit these gurdwaras by forming jathas of pilgrims.

---

[33] The Ardās is a set prayer in Sikhism. It is a part of worship service in a Gurdwara, daily rituals such as the opening the Sri Guru Granth Sahib or closing it in larger Gurdwaras, closing of congregational worship in smaller Gurdwaras, rites-of-passages such as with the naming of child or the cremation of a loved one, daily prayer by devout Sikhs and any significant Sikh ceremonies.

A few years after 1947, after the most iconic Sikh religious musician of Pakistan, Bhai Chand, had committed suicide, some lesser-known kirtanias, formerly of Amritsar, like Bhai Lal Junior, Bhai Ghulam Mohammad Chand Junior, and Bhai Sudarshan were alive and were quickly prepared by Pakistan to perform shabad kirtan at the historic gurdwaras. Also, for performing the priestly duties, Bhai Hari Singh was persuaded to become a fully practising Sikh all over again. He was then officially designated as the head priest of Gurdwara Janam Asthan at Nankana Sahib and was sent on special assignments to the other gurdwaras in Pakistan also. He also gave commentaries on Sikh history and on other subjects at Radio Pakistan Lahore's Punjabi Darbar service which could be heard in India as well. His mentor on gurbani and Sikh history was Giani Obaidullah of Radio Pakistan.

The *langar*[34] duties relating to hospitality for the Sikh visitors from India and the Sikh diaspora from the other countries were entrusted to the Guru Nanak Naam Lewa Sindhi Hindus/Sikhs based mostly in Karachi, Nawabshah, Sakhar and Hyderabad. Initially, the SGPC based in Amritsar had the de-facto control of all celebrations in various historic gurdwaras of Pakistan. For special occasions like Guru Nanak's birth anniversary celebrations in Nankana Sahib, Maharaja Ranjit Singh's birth and death anniversaries, the fifth Guru, Arjan Dev's martyrdom anniversary in Lahore, and Baisakhi35 celebrations at Panja Sahib in Hassan Abdal, the priests and musicians of the SGPC were sent from Amritsar to Pakistan. They were entrusted with the task of holding the non-stop recital from the Guru Granth Sahib (*akhand paath*) and shabad kirtan on all the

[34] The community kitchen of a gurdwara, which serves meals to all free of charge, regardless of religion.

[35] The day on which the community of amritdhari Sikhs was created in 1699.

special occasions. The rababi kirtanis of Pakistan played second fiddle to the visitors from India. From the music that was performed after 1947 in Nankana Sahib, it can be concluded that the old traditions of Gurdwara Janam Asthan have ceased to exist in Pakistan. Most of the musicians now performing shabad kirtan in Nankana Sahib on special occasions are either from the present crop of musicians of the Golden Temple or the Muslim rababi kirtanias who had been displaced in 1947 from Amritsar. The rababi Muslim musicians in Pakistan have lost touch with gurbani for more than 70 years. Some of them are too old and incapable of singing and performing religious duties, while others have died. It is time, thus, that Pakistan prepares a new generation of Sikh religious musicians from within.

After the creation of Pakistan, some of the Sikhs from West Punjab settled in far off states like West Bengal and Bihar. For those Sikhs settled in and around Patna, the birthplace of the tenth master, Guru Gobind Singh ji, some good Sikh religious musicians started serving in Takhat Sri Patna Sahib. One such outstanding group consisted of Bhai Gurbachan Singh and Joginder Singh. Similarly, some great musicians from time to time served in Takhat Sri Huzoor Sahib in Nanded. One such jatha consisted of Bhai Joginder Singh and Mohinder Singh of Nankana Sahib.

Today, Delhi is doing well as a centre of Sikh religious music because it has a greater Sikh population than any city in Punjab. The Delhi Sikhs are more well off too. I have concluded that the taste of Delhi Sikhs is also very rich, perhaps due to the fact that they were repetitively exposed to good quality Sikh religious music. Therefore, as things stand today, Delhi is leading the way in the fine art of gurdwara music in India. I have observed that the taste of the music of the Sikh *sangat*[36] in the United Kingdom, the United States

[36] Congregation.

of America, and Malaysia is also very high. Some of them have migrated from East Africa.

Some of the Sikhs in Malaysia are seriously involved in the process of preservation of vintage recordings of gurmat sangeet. There is an organisation called Kirtan Sewa of Malaysia, which used to invite top-grade Sikh religious musicians from India to Kuala Lumpur. These musicians were especially requested to present their finest pieces of music before the knowledgeable audiences. High-powered, wide-range (capable of recording the lowest to highest notes) microphones were used to record their music. This music was recorded onto cassette tapes and later on compact discs and pen-drives. Most of their music is now available on YouTube also. One of their pioneering *sewadars*[37] has been Ameer Singh. He sent special requests to the other lovers of Sikh religious music all over the world to share their personal collections with him.

When I was in the United States from 1980 to 2015, I also did some sewa at New Jersey's oldest Gurdwara Bridgewater, in Somerset County, from 1982 to 1999. During this period some of the finest Sikh religious musicians of India were invited to the gurdwara and their best renditions were recorded. Some of the most notable musicians among them have been Bhai Avtar Singh and Gurcharan Singh (1982, 1985, 1989, 1991, 1993, 1995), Bhai Shamsher Singh Zakhmi of Jalandhar and Bhai Mohan Pal Singh of Nankana Sahib and Patiala (1983), Bhai Didar Singh of village Nangal Khurd, district Hoshiarpur (1984-85), and Bhai Dilbagh Singh and Gulbagh Singh. Later, Bhai Nirmal Singh Khalsa, Bhai Gurmeet Singh Shant, Bhai Sarbjit Singh Rangeela, and Bhai Harjinder Singh of Srinagar also visited the USA.

---

[37] Those who render service or sewa.

2

Bhai Jwala Singh

An Icon of Pure Sikh Music

Half a millennium ago, what at present is a small, sleepy town called Sultanpur Lodhi, used to be a flourishing garrison town of the Lodhi Muslim dynasty that ruled northern India prior to the Mughal emperor Zaheer-ud-Din Babar's conquests. This small place was the seat of a provincial capital, other than Lahore and Sirhind, and was also a decently-sized trading and commercial centre. During those days, the present day big urban agglomerations of Punjab like Ludhiana, Jalandhar, Sialkot, Gujranwala and Amritsar were in existence, not as megacities and business centres, but in the form of small nondescript villages or clusters of villages located amidst fertile agricultural flatlands through which the five perennial rivers flowed.

Located on the eastern bank of the Ravi, the ancient city of Lahore was the biggest and most important regional administrative centre of the area north of capital Delhi. After Babar defeated the emperor of northern India, Ibrahim Khan Lodhi, in 1526 at the famous Battle of Panipat, Sultanpur Lodhi, which was governed by his kin, Daulat Khan Lodhi, also started falling on bad days. However, Sultanpur Lodhi stayed as an educational centre imparting Islamic education.

Babar and the subsequent Mughal rulers paid scant attention to Sultanpur Lodhi and virtually abandoned it. Sirhind became the most favoured town of the Mughals. However, prior to the Mughal Army's invasion and the conquest of northern India by Babar, Guru Nanak blessed Sultanpur Lodhi with his holy stay that exceeded 14 years. All his udasis started in Sultanpur. The spiritual foundation of the modern religion, called Sikhism, was laid by Guru Nanak in Sultanpur Lodhi and now, after five centuries, this town is a sacred centre of Sikh pilgrimage. During the second half of the eighteenth century, Nawab Jassa Singh Ahluwalia of Kapurthala annexed Sultanpur Lodhi. After that several gurdwaras associated with the memory of Guru Nanak were built in this town.

Bhai Jwala Singh and Party

Sultanpur Lodhi is surrounded by several small villages and Saidpur, near Thatha Tibba, is one of these. Situated on a dusty cart road, in ancient days Saidpur used to be a predominantly Muslim village with a small sprinkling of Sanatan Dharam Hindu population. Later, most of the Hindu families in and around Saidpur became the followers of Guru Nanak and during the period of the tenth master Guru Gobind Singh ji and afterwards during the reign of the Ahluwalia Misl, most of the Sikhs in the area grew unshorn hair and got baptized as amritdhari Sikhs. Yet, in population, the Muslims were outnumbering them till August 1947.

According to Bhai Avtar Singh, one of the ancestors of Bhai Jwala Singh was a follower of Guru Nanak and learnt the original Sikh religious music, gurmat sangeet, from the court of the tenth master, Guru Gobind Singh ji, obviously from the finest traditional rababi kirtanias of the time. Later, this meticulously-trained Sikh religious musician moved back to his native village, Fateabad in the Amritsar district and then to Saidpur in Kapurthala.

Bhai Jwala Singh (or Bhai Jawala Singh) was a proud descendant of the same blessed musician. Born in an area where the dhrupad style of North Indian classical music was still alive, he died as a genuine dhrupadia, unaffected by the khayali style. He mastered almost all the ancient taals which he played on the tabla and the pakhawaj, and also knew more than 500 tunes in all the 31 raagas that is mentioned in the Sri Guru Granth Sahib ji just like his ancestors of the past fifteen or so generations had known.

The Sikh religious music of ancient times was precisely composed in the dhrupad or the dhamar style. The most commonly followed taals of those days were dhrupad, dhamar, *panj taal, chaar taal, roopak taal, jhap taal, deep chandi, chhotti teen taal, waddi teen taal, ek taal (yakka), suhlfag taal, dadra,* and *kehrwa*. Some of these taals are sadly getting extinct now all over India. In some musical compositions of those days, several taals were used in sequences while rendering the same shabad. This unique style of music is called the partal format and was very effective in conveying the message of the Guru to audiences in several permutations and combinations of musical beats. Knowledgeable listeners, especially professional singers, used to appreciate the intricacies of this unique format. Unfortunately, this format of gurmat sangeet, too, is fast becoming extinct. In his days, Bhai Jwala Singh was a crusader for the preservation of the music of the era of the great Gurus.

Both big cities of the area, Amritsar and Lahore, became the leading centres of the newly evolving or experimental music. Evolution of the khayal format of classical music, which is the most prevalent these days, was underway since the days of the tenth master, Guru Gobind Singh ji, more than three centuries ago, but it was not accepted in the historic gurdwaras around Amritsar until the beginning of the twentieth century. At present, even the Sikh classical musicians render gurbani in the khayal format.

There were some places like Goindwal Sahib, Khadoor Sahib, Tarn Taran, Kapurthala and Sultanpur Lodhi, where khayal gayaki mostly came into prominence after the 1947 division of Punjab when rababi and other kirtanias from Nankana Sahib and other gurdwaras on both sides of the Radcliffe Line spread their favourite form of the khayal and thumri style of music in East Punjab.

While Bhai Jwala Singh's contemporaries, based in the bigger centres of music, like Amritsar, Lahore and Nankana Sahib, adopted khayal gayaki during the beginning of the twentieth century, Bhai Jwala Singh stood his ground and never abandoned the ancient dhrupad style. He was so unique that some of the rababi singers of Kapurthala, Goindwal Sahib, Jalandhar and Tarn Taran used to sit amongst the audience to listen to the renditions of gurbani when Bhai Jwala Singh was singing. Later, after listening to him, the rababi kirtanias used to personally express their appreciation to the unique icon of dhrupad shaili. In real life, Bhai Jwala Singh was a highly contented family man. He never ventured after money, and his diet was very simple, just like in a typical Guru ka langar. He was a very strict *nitnemi.*[38] He could miss other things but not his *nitnem.*[39]

Bhai Jwala Singh was born in 1872 in Saidpur or some nearby village in the Sultanpur Lodhi area. By the age of 12, he had crammed up the five baanis of the nitnem and several hundred shabads contained in holy Sri Guru Granth Sahib.

His first *ustad*[40] was his own father, Bhai Deva Singh, who taught him the rendition of gurbani in a number of original reets that were prevalent in gurmat sangeet of the times of the Guru darbars. Later, his father sent him for more coaching to learn the more intricate points of gurmat sangeet from another highly accomplished dhrupad style kirtanya, Bhai Sardha Singh. His third ustad was a strict dhrupadia trainer – Bhai Wasawa Singh (popularly known as Bhai Rangi Ram). Bhai Rangi Ram was a disciplinarian in the application of grammar of ancient music and he mostly stayed in Tarn Taran. All three of his ustads were adept in the rendition of the gurbani in its pristine originality which dated back to the times of the great Gurus.

By the age of 20, Bhai Jwala Singh had become an accomplished kirtania of the Guru's word in the Guru's own shaili of rendition. His fame spread far and wide and he was in great demand in all the villages and towns of the princely state of Kapurthala and the neighbouring British-ruled districts of Amritsar, Ferozepore, Lahore, Hoshiarpur, Ludhiana and Jalandhar.

In addition to culturing his vocal cords for the dhrupad-based gurmat sangeet, Bhai Jwala Singh became an

---

[38] One who does his *nitnem* regulalrly. See note below.

[39] Daily recital of the five baanis (Sikh hymns) of the Gurus.

[40] Mentor and teacher, especially a musician.

accomplished tabla player as well. He could play at least two popular string instruments – the taus and the saranda – before switching to the immensely popular and easy-to-play harmonium. Sometimes, the mridang or the pakhawaj accompanied Bhai Jwala Singh during his classical renditions.

The old guards of dhrupad based gurmat sangeet were leaving this world one by one and there were no replacements in the pipeline. It was only in the 1920s that Bhai Jwala Singh began to get acknowledged as the finest living dhrupadia kirtania of the Sikh community. His peculiar rich, vibratory and voluminous voice had a distinct ringing sound, which made him stand apart amongst all his contemporaries. Some people believe that when the Late Kundan Lal Saigal sang his most memorable numbers for the film *Tansen,* in the mid-1940s, he took inspiration from the style of Bhai Jwala Singh. K.L. Saigal had, in his younger years, listened to the shabad kirtan by Bhai Jwala Singh in Jalandhar, Amritsar or somewhere else in the area. The other great maestros of the time like Dilip Chandra Vedi also listened to him.

As early as 1890, Bhai Jwala Singh had come to be recognised as the leading kirtania in and around Sultanpur Lodhi. He became a regular performer of shabad kirtan at Gurdwaras Sri Ber Sahib and Sri Hat Sahib within the town of Sultanpur Lodhi.

Bhai Jwala Singh's contemporary ruler of the Princely State of Kapurthala was Maharaja Jagatjit Singh. He was not a practising Sikh, but nevertheless was an admirer of classical music. During the 1930s, he built an architectural marvel – the State Gurdwara Sahib of Kapurthala. When the first *parkash*[41] of Sri Guru Granth Sahib was done in this gurdwara, Bhai Jwala Singh was specially invited to perform the shabad kirtan in the inaugural program. He often

[41] Ritual ceremony for the installing the Sri Guru Granth Sahib ji.

performed 'Asa Di Vaar' and evening chowkis of shabad kirtan there too.

Many Sikh courtiers of the Maharaja, including my late father, were great admirers of Bhai Jwala Singh and they all patronised him. Even the Muslims of Kapurthala were great appreciative of the music and other qualities of Bhai Jwala Singh. The Muslim Commanding Officer of the Kapurthala State Forces, Colonel Asghar Ali Khan, had become a great admirer of Bhai Jwala Singh ji's musical genius. One day he told my father to invite either Bhai Jwala Singh of Sultanpur Lodhi or Bhai Santa Singh of the Golden Temple to his house and he (Asghar Ali) would cancel all engagement to listen to their kirtan. Asghar Ali Khan used to give ten rupees (in the 1930s and 1940s) to Bhai Jwala Singh, whenever he attended his kirtan. So did Diwan Jarmani Dass, another top bureaucrat of the Kapurthala state.

Bhai Jwala Singh never served the *mahant*[42] managers of the historic gurdwaras or their successor, the SGPC, but he was often invited to perform Gurpurb specials at the Golden Temple in Amritsar, Sri Darbar Sahib at Tarn Taran, and the other historic gurdwaras at Khadoor Sahib, Baba Bakala, Chheharta, Basarke Gillan, and Goindwal Sahib. Bhai Jwala Singh was very popular amongst the *sardars (jagirdars)*[43] of Kapurthala and he was in great demand in Patti, Sarhali, Khemkaran, Bhikhiwind, Ferozepore and Kasur.

Sham Churasi is a small village known for its traditions of classical music. At one time, during the nineteenth century, this village had the distinction of producing some of the finest dhrupadia singers of Punjab, but when its most famous sons, Nazaqat Ali and Salamat Ali Khan, came on the scene, they made a complete departure from the past and

---

[42] Hereditary managers who controlled and held the door keys of Sikh gurudwaras.

[43] Landlords.

decided to excel in khayal gayaki. However, the most knowledgeable old-timers in the village always loved to listen to the dhrupads and dhamars of Bhai Jwala Singh whenever he visited their village in the Hoshiarpur district.

Even iconic kirtanias of his time, like Bhai Mehar, Bhai Lal Senior, Bhai Chand, Bhai Faiz and Bhai Santa Singh, all hazoori raagis of the Golden Temple, held Bhai Jwala Singh in very high esteem and they listened to his renditions with the utmost respect and reverence.

When Maharaja Bhupinder Singh of Patiala came to know about the unique knowledge of ancient music and other qualities of Bhai Jwala Singh, he decided to use his services to teach the dhrupad format of classical music to some selected musicians of his Patiala Gharan, like Mahant Gajja Singh. The Maharaja also wanted his musicians to learn to play the taus and the saranda from him.

This gharana had earned a lot of name and fame in India, but it was a khayal-centric gharana with thumri and dadra as the semi-classical 'side-kicks' introduced by Bade Ghulam Ali Khan and his younger brother, Barqat Ali Khan.

Like a highly motivated student, in addition to mastering the two string instruments, Mahant Gajja Singh also learnt the subtle intricacies of the dhrupad style of classical singing from Bhai Jwala Singh. On learning about the new achievements of Mahant Gajja Singh, the Maharaja became very happy and as a token of gratitude, he showered expensive gifts on him.

By nature, Bhai Jwala Singh was a shy and non-political person. But at one time, the prevailing unfavourable working conditions for the performers of gurmat sangeet compelled him to form a union of the kirtanias. Being a freelancer kirtania himself, Bhai Jwala Singh fought like a soldier for the rights of his fellow gurmat sangeet professionals and succeeded in winning a number of concessions from the

SGPC. Even the kirtanias serving the numerous Singh Sabhas in Punjab, the Princely State of Kashmir and Northwest Frontier Province, benefited from the concessions negotiated by Bhai Jwala Singh. When the Singh Sabha Movement for the liberation of the historic gurdwaras was launched towards the end of World War II, Bhai Jwala Singh took an active part in it and was imprisoned too as a part of the Jaito Morcha, Guru Ka Baag Morcha and Nankana Sahib Morcha. During this prolonged agitation, he suffered financially too, but his steadfast faith in the movement was never shaken. He never demanded money for performing shabad kirtan. Whatever the hosts offered him, was accepted as the Guru's *kripa*.[44]

Just like his predecessors, Bhai Jwala Singh also found it appropriate to teach all that he had learnt from his illustrious father and other famous ustads to his young sons, Bhai Gurcharan Singh and Bhai Avtar Singh. Both brothers learnt virtually all 500 gurmat sangeet reets from their father.

Bhai Jwala Singh's raagi jatha was not confined to just three musicians. Sometimes he had a chorus group of eight to ten musicians performing shabad kirtan while at other times he had one taus and two sarandas as accompaniments. The effect of the gurmat sangeet chorus of Bhai Jwala Singh and his party was simply mesmerising. Both his sons were with their father's group from the 1930s. When Bhai Jwala Singh switched to the harmonium as his main musical instrument around the time of the First World War, between 1914 and 1919, most of his contemporaries were doing so as well.

Bhai Jwala Singh had a unique style of all-night *rain-sabhai kirtan* singing. On several occasions, his large group of musicians would start the rendition of the complete kirtan of Sukhmani Sahib around 8 p.m. and the singing went on and

[44] Grace.

on till about 5 a.m. of the following morning. This special chowki of shabad kirtan was called *Sukhmana*. The rendition started with the raagas that were appropriate for the first *pehar*[45] of the night and went on to the raagas of the second pehar and then the rest in chronological order.

Bhai Jwala Singh always strictly adhered to the proper timings of the raagas. During the non-stop renditions of Sukhmana, the lead singer, as well as the others, could only briefly leave the chowki for partaking in food and other essential activities during which time the others took over. Timewise, this was a very lengthy and difficult undertaking, but the raagis of those days were quite proficient in completing the entire Sukhmani Sahib that lasted for several hours without interruption. These days, I don't think any musician will be able to perform the complete Sukhmana like Bhai Jwala Singh used to.

His sons had once told me that in their younger years, even they used to render the complete Sukhmana in one night-long sitting. They were both very good at the grammar of music. During the 1990s, Bhai Gurcharan Singh was getting old and began experiencing difficulties in sitting. That's when Bhai Avtar Singh took over the jatha. After a serious illness, on 24 November 2006, Bhai Avtar Singh left for his heavenly abode. Bhai Gurcharan Singh died at the age of 102 on 12 November 2017. For about five years, from 1947 to 1952, Bhai Swarn Singh, the son of Bhai Jwala Singh's older son, Mela Singh, served as his tabla player, having learnt all the taals used in gurmat sangeet.

People like my father who had heard Bhai Jwala Singh claim that his voice was unique and better than that of his sons, but in the absence of any recordings, we don't know as to how great he was. It's a pity! I asked my father why shabad

---

[45] The *pehar* consists of three hours and the names and the nature of renditions of the raagas change after each pehar.

kirtan rendered by Bhai Jwala Singh was never recorded. He told me that the Genophone Recording Company, owned by Janki Nath Kumar and brothers, was active in Lahore since the early 1930s, and His Master's Voice opened its doors in Lahore in 1941. For Bhai Jwala Singh, who was based at Sultanpur Lodhi, it was a four-hour journey by rail or road to Lahore and the timings of the trains and buses were unsuitable. There was an hourly bus service between Sultanpur Lodhi and Kapurthala and a one-and-a-half hourly service between Kapurthala and Amritsar. The trains were even fewer and were running at inconvenient times. Most probably, inadequate connectivity between Sultanpur Lodhi and Lahore was responsible for his not recording his renditions. The All India Radio in Lahore, which opened in 1937, had the facility of transcription service on 12-inch diameter 78-RPM records, but Bhai Jwala Singh somehow never expressed his desire to perform at the Lahore radio station.

Even as a kirtania, Bhai Jwala Singh owned some agricultural land in the Saidpur village where, in his spare time, he grew crops. Sugarcane was the family's favourite crop and they enjoyed making jaggery from it. Growing wheat was their second love. They owned milch cattle too. Suddenly in 1947, communal riots erupted all over Punjab. The Muslims were in majority in most of the villages around Sultanpur Lodhi, but when it was confirmed that Kapurthala along with Amritsar was not going to Pakistan, the Muslims got subdued and the Sikhs became aggressive. As a disciple of the Guru, Bhai Jwala Singh rescued several Muslims and sheltered them in his spacious home, until such time that the army evacuated them and took them to Pakistan.

Bhai Jwala Singh bought some land in the Jatt Sikh dominated village of Bhulana on the Kapurthala-Sultanpur Lodhi Road, where the traditional farmers did not allow the non-agriculturists communities to buy agricultural land. No one came forward to till their land even on rent. In utter frustration, Bhai Jwala Singh complained to my father who was the Inspector General of Kapurthala State Police then. On his strong interjection, the Jatt Sikhs relented and from then on, his land was cultivated on rent.

After the division of Punjab in 1947, the first pair of radio stations in East Punjab opened in 1948. The Jalandhar studio of All India Radio was less than 30 miles from Sultanpur Lodhi and the connectivity by train and road was also better, but by that time Bhai Jwala Singh had grown very old and his health was also not too good. So, he allowed his sons to explore the avenue of singing for the radio, but he stayed away from it for as long as he lived.

Around 1951, when All India Radio Jalandhar-Amritsar was barely two years old, the two brothers Bhai Avtar Singh and Gurcharan Singh applied for an audition at the new radio station. It was no surprise that both were approved. Around that time, Bhai Jwala Singh felt that he was getting old, and so he started encouraging his sons to form their own independent kirtan jatha too.

Approximately at the age of 80, Bhai Jwala Singh left for his heavenly abode on 29 May 1952. However, his sons, and now one of his grandsons, Bhai Kultar Singh, are carrying on his traditions in letter and spirit. After Bhai Jwala Singh's death, Bhai Swarn Singh joined the jatha of Bhai Avtar Singh and Gurcharan Singh. He is now the drummer with the jatha of Bhai Kultar Singh.

3

Bhai Samund Singh

The Hazoori Raagi and Heavenly Minstrel

'So kyon visre meri maye' was a shabad being rendered on the radio in a highly emotional tone and texture by an unheard of but extraordinary singer. His highly cultured voice completely mesmerised me when I tuned into All India Radio Jalandhar-Amritsar one day way back in 1952. Later, a voice-over announced: 'You have just heard the voice of Bhai Samund Singh Ragi singing a shabad.'

My father, during the years of his college, had heard this magical and emotive voice for the first time in the mid-1920s at Gurdwara Janam Asthan Sri Nankana Sahib, during the marathon celebrations of the Birth Anniversary of Guru Nanak. Since that moment, he had become a lifelong admirer of Bhai Samund Singh. With extreme reverence, he would refer to him as a *samundar* of gurmat sangeet (an ocean of Sikh religious music).

In my case, too, from that morning of 1952, I became a big fan of the sweet, melodious and enchanting voice of Bhai Samund Singh. Whenever he happened to visit the studios of All India Radio Jalandhar, he was accorded the respect he amply deserved. The authorities of All India Radio Jalandhar-Amritsar fixed the Friday of every week for shabad kirtan programmes at the radio station. Bhai Samund Singh was invited at least once every fortnight to perform live at Punjab's only radio station.

This radio station had a large number of its own musical instruments, including several tanpuras.[46] Bhai Samund Singh and Master Rattan of Phagwara were always requested to choose any one of the tanpuras for accompaniment, while most other musicians had to bring their own tanpuras. One of the staff artists, an accomplished clarinet player, had become a big fan of Bhai Samund Singh. He always insisted on accompanying Bhai *Sahib* during his shabad kirtan. Similarly, a violinist always showed eagerness in playing his instrument with Bhai Sahib. Such was his charisma!

These facts, and several others, were told to me by the late Sardar Jodh Singh, who retired as Assistant Station Director of All India Radio Jalandhar. During the twice-a-month visits to the radio station, he almost invariably invited Bhai Samund Singh to have lunch at his residence. They remained very good lifelong friends. He also told me that the ancestry and relatives of Bhai Samund Singh hailed from the districts of Sheikhupura, Gujranwala, Lyallpur and Montgomery.

Before independence and the tragic partition of Punjab, he had served as a headmaster at Lyallpur (now Faisalabad) in West Punjab. According to him, strict nitnem and

---

[46] *Tanpura:* It is a string instrument which accompanies every Sikh and sub-continental classical musician during the rendition of classical numbers

regular riyaz of the raagas was a hallmark of Bhai Samund Singh's lifestyle from childhood.

Bhai Samund Singh was born in 1900 in a relatively nondescript village called Mulla Hamza in Montgomery (now Sahiwal) district of West Punjab. This district was famous for its wealthy Sikh farming community and was one of the favoured districts of the British rulers. Although the Sikhs constituted barely ten per cent of the population of that district, yet financially they were very well off and controlled the economy of the area. It won't be incorrect to say that Sikhism thrived in this area of Multan division so much so that several Hindu families of the area used to convert their elder son to Sikhism.

One of the role models for the Sikh community of the area was the family of Bhai Huzoor Singh, the illustrious father of Bhai Samund Singh. When Samund was still very young, between the age of six to ten, Bhai Hazoor Singh had set a vigorous training regime for him. He was made to learn *Japji Sahib* and *Rehraas* by heart by the time he turned ten. By the age of 12, Samund Singh had learnt at least 1,000 shabads from the Guru Granth by heart. He had also undergone proper introductory training in several commonly sung gurmat sangeet and other raagas by that age.

Thenceforth, training in the raagas and mastering their technique became a lifelong obsession for the young musician. Even while lying in bed, he would have his tanpura by his side. He experimented with singing each shabad in several raagas and taals. Some of the raagas were prescribed in the Guru Granth – some were similar in *thath*,[47] and some were purely based on the time of the day and mood when the verse was being sung.

---

[47] Essence.

The family lived and served in the historic shrines at Nankana Sahib, the birthplace of Guru Nanak, located in the Sheikhpura district of Lahore Division and the neighbourhood. At the age of 12, Samund Singh would perform at least one of the several chowkis of shabad kirtan every day at Gurdwara Nankana Sahib.

The then hereditary managers of the shrine were called mahants. They had a host of failings which have been highlighted in several written documents. They had many weaknesses in their opulent lifestyles, but they also had something good to their credit. They were quite knowledgeable about Sikh religious music. They knew the correct structure of the raagas, and they could quickly distinguish between an accomplished raagi and one who wasn't. One such manager discovered the extraordinary talent in young Samund Singh and offered him a permanent position as the hazoori kirtania at the famous Sikh shrine.

Bhai Samund Singh was essentially an exponent of the khayal shaili school of shabad kirtan. He did sing some dhrupads too, which, due to his great voice and easy modulation, were considered masterpieces.

By the middle of the nineteenth century, most of the rababi kirtanyas had mastered the khayal shaili tradition. However, they had the tendency of extending the khayal format too long and wide. They started with a long alaap (without starting the drumbeat) and gradually went into jorh alaap, before starting the rendition of the shabad in vilambhat lai and then warming up to madh lai and finally going into the fast climax tempo called dhrutt lai. While doing the dhrutt lai, many times the wording of the gurbani became less clear.

Bhai Samund Singh gave utmost importance to the clarity of the words of gurbani. He mastered a new format. After a short alaap, he used to go directly into the madh lai and completed the entire shabad in the same tempo. Most of the time, he completely omitted the dhrutt lai. This resulted in a marked clarity in the words, which was also the aim of the Gurus. Bhai Samund Singh's style of rendition was named *chhota raaga shaili*. Despite his innovation, the rababi kirtanias continued to follow the longer khayal shaili format.

The rababis would indulge in a lot of unnecessary exhibitions of their skills during rendition called taan paltas. This kind of practice was alien to Bhai Samund Singh. For him, his ultimate master, the Guru, was supreme and the raaga was subservient to the Guru's message.

From 1912 till August 1947, Bhai Samund Singh served as a hazoori raagi. After 1935, he became the leading hazoori raagi at the Janam Asthan.

During his service at Nankana Sahib, he met a number of well-known kirtanias, many of whom were rababis who were considered masters of North Indian classical music. His interaction with them was extremely useful to both. Each one learnt something new from the vast reservoir of knowledge attained by the other. Among some of his contemporary rababis were Bhai Tana Singh, Bhai Gurmukh Singh Fakkar,

Bhai Sarmukh Singh Fakkar, Bhai Pall Singh, and Bhai Jaswant Singh, to name a few. Some rababis, though, had retained their Islamic names and were not practising Sikhs. They included Bhai Naseera, Bhai Sudarshan and Bhai Rashida. On special occasions, some rababis used to come from Amritsar to perform at various gurdwaras in Nankana Sahib. They included Bhai Chanan, Bhai Mehar, Bhai Faiz, Bhai Lal, Bhai Chand, and Bhai Taba.

In 1925, through British-Indian legislation, the duly-elected SGPC came into existence. It was headquartered in the Darbar Sahib Complex in Amritsar, and had jurisdiction over most of the historic Sikh shrines located in the Punjab provinces and North-West Frontier Province (NWFP), including Nankana Sahib. The new committee quickly went to work and made several changes, including the rotation of raagi jathas from one historic shrine to the other.

During this time, Bhai Samund Singh also started travelling a lot. The rich Sikh sangat of Lyallpur, Sri Ganganagar and Montgomery was always pleased to invite Bhai Samund Singh to perform shabad kirtan in the local gurdwaras at Lyallpur, Montgomery, Sri Ganganagar, Tobha Tek Singh, Samundri, Okarha, Mandi Burewal and Gojra, to name a few. There were some very staunch Sikhs living in far-flung areas of the North-West Frontier Province, Balochistan and Sindh. They would also invite Bhai Samund Singh to their gurdwaras. This spread his name and fame in faraway places. Members of the Sikh community, wherever he went, gave him a lot of love and respect.

At Nankana Sahib, the longest and the most demanding shabad chowki was for the singing of the morning's 'Asa Di Vaar'. Starting well before sunrise and ending at dawn, it lasted for at least two hours. After 1935, Bhai Samund Singh was accorded more slots each month to perform it. He discharged this duty with utmost devotion and reverence. He mastered the technique of the rendering of 'Asraje Tunde Di Dhuni' to perfection. I have heard 'Asa Di Vaar' sung by Bhai Santa Singh, Bhai Samund Singh, and Bhai Budh Singh Taan. As far as the 'Asraje Tunde Di Dhuni' is concerned, all three are quite identical. Bhai Santa Singh's tempo was slightly faster though. Also, he was very particular about the timing of the raaga, and rarely made a variation from their strict time regime. Today, though, if we listen to the present-day kirtanias at the Darbar Sahib, we see that there is no standardisation of 'Asraje Tunde Di Dhuni' anymore.

All India Radio Lahore, the then sole radio station in Punjab, opened a state-of-the-art studio complex in 1937. This radio station needed a host of artists of all kinds. In the religious category, they needed Muslim *naat* and *qawwali* singers, Sikh gurmat sangeet singers, and Hindu bhajan singers. Bhai Samund Singh of Nankana Sahib and Bhai Santa Singh of the Darbar Sahib were approved as the staff artists in the very first year. Soon they both attained the A-Class in their category. These two stalwarts had contrasting styles. Bhai Santa Singh sang invariably in very high notes, but Bhai Samund Singh always sang in a completely relaxed

Bhai Samudh Singh Ragi and Party will broadcast Shabd from Lahore on October 7.

style in all kinds of notes, and seldom went into the highest ones. Bhai Santa Singh mostly sang in kehrwa taal and laid utmost stress on his highly cultured voice, but Bhai Samund Singh used most of the taals used by the contemporary and old Sikh musicians. Through prolonged riyaz, Bhai Samund Singh had developed such a fine *murki*[48] in his voice that he could render the most difficult modulations with perfect ease. A lot of musicians tried to imitate him but could not.

At All India Radio Lahore, Bhai Samund Singh met all-time great maestros like Bade Ghulam Ali Khan, Vinayak Rao Patwardhan, Dalip Singh Bedi, Barqat Ali Khan, Din Mohammad, Kallan Khan, Harish Chander Bali, and Master Rattan. Between performances and afterwards, they used to run into each other. Each one of them was not afraid of asking the other about the finer points of classical music. These discussions sometimes led to heated discussions, too, but soon every difference used to be resolved amicably.

Bhai Samund Singh used to commute at least once every month to Lahore from Nankana Sahib. In the same way, Bhai Santa Singh used to commute from Amritsar to Lahore. Bhai Sudh Singh and Pradhan Singh were also later approved as radio singers. A local artist, Bhai Budh Singh Taan, was the only approved radio singer, who used to perform shabad kirtan as a solo artist.

While in Lahore, Bhai Samund Singh used to stay overnight at Gurdwara Dehra Sahib and used to perform a chowki there. Whenever his voice was heard over the airwaves, the evening crowds at Dehra Sahib would invariably swell to several times the normal attendance. Among the listeners would be many Muslims, Hindus and Christians. Music Director Vinod was one of the Christians who used to listen to Bhai Samund Singh at Dehra Sahib.

In order to stay within their time constraints, All India

---

[48] Murki is a short taan or inverted mordent in Hindustani classical music.

Radio Lahore used to determine the time limit of the shabad to be sung. Bhai Samund Singh, during rehearsal, used to sing each stanza at least once and if he could not complete the entire shabad within the stipulated time slot, he would refuse to sing that shabad for the radio. It is a principle of not leaving any part of a shabad unsung. His strict gurmat principles were always his strength and the authorities of All India Radio never defied him.

On the radio, Bhai Samund Singh would utilise the minimum possible time for singing shabads, but while performing in the gurdwaras, he was more relaxed and he took more time to sing the same shabad, thus doing full justice to each *elahi* (Godly) word.

Bhai Vir Singh, the great poet laureate of Punjabi, was very much opposed to *katha*[49] by kirtanias too. He believed that katha should be the domain of the *kathakars,*[50] as much as the kathakars should leave the art of singing of the shabad to the kirtanias. Each can do a better job in their field of speciality. Bhai Samund Singh agreed with Bhai Vir Singh's advice – he was against having katha while doing kirtan.

Thumri is a semi-classical form of classical music. It took a concrete shape during the mid-nineteenth century. It conveys, in a most effective manner, the subtle emotions of love, devotion and the pangs of separation from the lover. Gurbani, too, has numerous shabads conveying similar emotions; the only difference being that in Gurbani, love and devotion are directed towards the Almighty.

The thumri had not been a form of music in Punjab until the second decade of the twentieth century. In fact, Bade Ghulam Ali Khan, a contemporary and a good friend of Bhai Samund Singh, perfected the Punjabi version of the singing

---

[49] Katha is the verbal explanation/discourse of Gurbani (the utterings of the Guru's).

[50] interpreters of the Guru's word

at the time of the creation of thumri during the 1930s and 1940s. He recorded his best renditions of thumris in the 1940s. Bhai Samund Singh selectively adopted the thumri style, and this innovation found its acceptance by the Sikhs in overwhelming numbers. Some of such shabads were originally sung at All India Radio Lahore. During those days, tape recordings and transcripts of programmes were not made by All India Radio, hence none of them is available anymore. Bhai Gurmeet Singh Shant of Jalandhar has, in recent years, adopted the thumri for some of his tunes and the Sikh community has welcomed them.

It was the communal frenzy and bloodshed of horrific proportions at the time of the creation of Pakistan that led the family of Bhai Samund Singh to leave their ancestral homes and hearths for good and migrate to the holy city of Amritsar. Such decisions are rather tough to make, especially when you have spent your entire life serving at the birthplace of the founder of your faith.

Soon after independence and the partition of Punjab into Indian (East) Punjab and Pakistani (West) Punjab), Bhai Samund Singh camped in Amritsar, where he took on the position of hazoori raagi at the Darbar Sahib. Another brilliant contemporary of his, Bhai Chand, a rababi Muslim kirtania, was still serving at the Darbar Sahib but was ready to leave for Pakistan. After going to Pakistan, Bhai Chand became a lonely and disgraced person, who eventually could not adjust to his new circumstances. Eventually, frustrated and financially broken, he tragically committed suicide.

Within a couple of years, Bhai Samund Singh decided to become a freelance raagi and shifted his residence to Ludhiana, where he lived for the rest of his life.

He became an A-class artist of All India Radio Jalandhar-Amritsar when this newly established radio station was commissioned in 1948. Most of the staff at this radio station had migrated from West Punjab and some had already served at All India Radio Lahore. For a short while, Sardar Kartar Singh Duggal, a veteran from All India Radio Lahore and Peshawar, served as a top official at this radio station. Sardar Jodh Singh, a refugee from Lyallpur and Gujjranwala, also joined as a producer of programmes in Punjabi here. Bhai Samund Singh was the most revered religious and classical musician at this station. Occasionally, he was also asked to perform at the Delhi and Lucknow stations of All India Radio.

Once while at the Delhi radio station, his talent caught the attention of the experts of classical music in the nation's capital. On their recommendation, Bhai Samund Singh got the unique distinction of becoming the first Sikh religious classical musician to perform a one-and-a-half-hour-long live programme in the prestigious weekly Akhil Bharatiya Programme of Classical Music on a Saturday evening. This special programme had a record listenership. He performed so well and with such remarkable ease that at the end of the programme, he was given a big ovation by all. After that, he started performing more frequently at All India Radio Delhi and other regional stations.

The Chief Khalsa Diwan in Amritsar, the premier institution that established the Khalsa College Amritsar and several other Sikh educational institutions, used to hold annual Sikh Educational Conferences. Bhai Samund Singh was always an invitee in those conferences, and he invariably was the official kirtania.

During the 1969 quincentennial celebration of the birth of Guru Nanak, a set of five long-playing records were released and Bhai Samund Singh was the most prominent singer featured on this one-of-a-kind set of records.

While serving in Nankana Sahib and singing in Lahore, Bhai Samund Singh was reluctant to allow cutting of gramophone discs of shabads rendered by him, but during the 1960s, his voice was featured prominently on several 33-RPM LP (long-playing) records. Some of his All India Radio performances were also recorded on professional fast-speed tapes.

During the 1960s, Professor Taaran Singh, one of the heads of departments at the Punjabi University in Patiala, wanted to record shabad kirtan in original vintage tunes by the great masters of Sikh religious music. He got especially worried after the untimely death of Bhai Santa Singh ji at age 62 in 1966. After obtaining due permission from the then Vice-Chancellor of the university, he got the project going. Among the first raagis he requested to record in their original reets was Bhai Samund Singh. Others included Bhai Dharam Singh Zakhmi.

Bhai Samund Singh recorded several shabads in his inimitable style. Later, he recommended that the vast reservoir of gurmat sangeet in ancient dhrupad and dhamar styles deserved preservation. On this suggestion, Professor Taaran Singh requested Bhai Avtar Singh and Bhai Gurcharan Singh, who were then serving in various historic gurdwaras of Delhi, to record in their original tunes for the Punjabi University Library at Patiala. Both told me that they recorded over 500 vintage tunes of shabad kirtan in their voices, accompanied by the tanpura. To the best of my knowledge, neither the recordings of Bhai Samund Singh nor those of Bhai Avtar Singh and Gurcharan Singh are now available with the university. Such is the pathetic state of storage and preservation in our universities today!

Sohan Singh Misha, a brilliant poet of Punjabi and an academician, served All India Radio Jalandhar in various capacities. Due to his brilliance, he rose to become the second senior-most official at this capital station. He was a blunt talker, too. Once he told me that he shuns religious activity in any form, but when Bhai Samund Singh sings, he is transported into a world of ecstasy and romanticism rarely experienced otherwise! He also said that it would have been better if Bhai Samund Singh would have been a ghazal singer too, as he would have then composed some very soulful verses for him. I advised him not to share these thoughts with Bhai Samund Singh, since he is a deeply pious man, and would be hurt by his frivolities.

The Pakistani Muslims who had heard Bhai Samund Singh over the airwaves before the partition of Punjab used to tune in to All India Radio Jalandhar to especially listen to his seasoned voice. It used to receive hundreds of letters from his fans from both sides of the new border.

A famous music director from Bollywood, Mohinder Singh Sarna, popularly known as S. Mohinder, once told me that he owed his career as a music director to Bhai Samund Singh. When he was a child, his father was posted as a prosecuting inspector in Lyallpur, where he was initiated into classical music by the late Sant Sujan Singh, a descendant of Baba Nand Singh. Later on, his father was posted at Sheikhpura and he came into contact with Bhai Samund Singh at the nearby town of Nankana Sahib. Here, young Mohinder became a pupil of Bhai Samund Singh, who taught him the basics of several commonly used classical raagas. These became a stepping stone for him in becoming a full-fledged Bollywood music director later in life.

The Punjabi film, *Nanak Naam Jahaz Hai,* was made in 1969 and was accorded the President of India's All India Gold Medal for excellence in film music. Although Mohammad Rafi and Asha Bhonsle also sang for this film, the most revered singer in the award-winning film was undoubtedly Bhai Samund Singh. His voice in the raagas of his choice was most prominently featured in two shabads sung for this film.

Towards the end of 1971, Bhai Samund Singh was a very sad grand old man of Sikh religious music. The public taste of the Sikh community had deteriorated significantly. Mediocrity had taken over in popular kirtan and those who had struggled hard to hone their skills in the raagas were being short-changed. Even the authorities running the historic Sikh shrines were quite indifferent to the merit of the hazoori raagis. When Bhai Avtar Singh, Gurcharan Singh and Swaran Singh went to see him during his final days, in frustration Bhai Samund Singh told them that the golden days of good musicians were over and that the SGPC was recruiting mediocre raagis and even the sangat was giving more importance to them at the expense of good ones.

In January 1972, after a bout of ill health, Bhai Samund Singh left for his heavenly abode. All India Radio has been quite irresponsible in preserving Bhai Samund Singh's voice. Hundreds of hours of his tape recordings were lying unprotected in the storage of All India Radio Jalandhar. Some of these tapes were later erased to be used for recording music of other, new artists. After his death, the authorities of the Punjab & Sind Bank approached All India Radio Jalandhar to make available all old recordings of Bhai Samund Singh for preserving his voice on long-playing records. They were given recordings for one and a half hours only! The rest of his music had been destroyed, due to callous negligence and lack of professionalism. Even his famous recording of 'Asa Di Vaar' by All India Radio Jalandhar has been lost forever. Had all

his recordings been preserved, we could have listened to hundreds of hours of his finest renditions. On the other hand, though, the Hindustan Recording Company of Calcutta has preserved the entire recording of the music of K.L. Saigal.

(Courtesy: *South Asia Post*, 1 May 2009)

4

Bhai Santa Singh

The Great Bard of Divine Music

As a child, I was used to waking up between 6-7 a.m., but on one cold winter morning of 1948, my mother woke me up at about 4:30 a.m., gave me a bath, and made my *joorrah*. After I was dressed, she took me to the radio and asked me to switch it on. I pushed the button, and the light came on. Soon, after the tubes warmed up, the sound appeared. Hearing the sign-on tune of All India Radio looked like a great achievement. A sweet voice announced the time as 5:00 a.m., and a special one-hour morning service on the airwaves of All India Radio Jalandhar-Amritsar in honour of the birth anniversary of Guru Nanak began.

The announcer said that the listeners would be taken to the Darbar Sahib in Amritsar for a direct transmission of the recitation of 'Asa Di Vaar' on the special occasion of the birth anniversary of Sri Guru Nanak Dev ji. Within seconds the beat of the tabla, the sound of the harmonium, and the high-pitched voices of a group of musicians could be heard. It seemed that the musicians were talking to the Guru, inviting Him to bless this Earth once again with His physical presence in human form.

The special recitation of the hymns of the Guru sounded genuinely emotional. At that young age I did not understand the meaning of the songs. Yet, I felt highly impressed by the melodious voice, tone and texture of the music. For a number of years thereafter, the voices heard on that day were shrouded in mystery, but my curiosity always remained to unravel it.

Several years later, I had a chance meeting in America with Sardar Jodh Singh, the retired Assistant Station Director of All India Radio Jalandhar. He happened to be the announcer of the programme in the sanctum sanctorum of the Golden Temple on that auspicious day. He revealed, for the first time, that the group of musicians performing the shabad kirtan during the first-ever live transmission from the Golden Temple was indeed led by the legendry Bhai Santa Singh, the then senior-most raagi at Harmandar Sahib. I had known it all along that it had been somebody special and highly accomplished.

Several shabads recorded on 78-RPM gramophone records by Bhai Santa Singh and his group were available in the market for decades, starting from the 1940s, and different stations of All India Radio including Delhi, Jalandhar, Jammu, and Lucknow used to play these records in their early morning programs of religious music.

Bhai Santa Singh had the God-given unique capability to sing in very high notes, almost resembling the voice of a female singer, which most other musicians could not replicate. This characteristic of his voice was resented by the other senior musicians of the Golden Temple who had heavy male voices. As a result, he was not allowed to perform shabad kirtan at the Golden Temple for many years. He was allowed to sing at Baba Atal Rai and the other smaller gurdwaras though. However, when Sikh scholars like Bhai Vir Singh and other knowledgeable listeners started giving him due respect, he got his chance to sing in the sanctum sanctorum of the Golden Temple. His fame soared higher when the experts of music at All India Radio Lahore gave him the status of an A-class artist and he was even invited to perform gurmat sangeet at All India Radio Peshawar.

His exact date of birth is not known, but according to recorded information he was born in the walled city of Amritsar in 1904. Some others think that he was born in 1912. During those days very few Sikhs used to sing even in the gurdwaras and those who did had to hone their skills in classical music under the strict guidance of mostly Muslims or pundits who were trained classical teachers.

Bhai Santa Singh was no exception. He enrolled at a very young age as a learner of Sikh classical music in the music department of the famous Yateemkhana in Amritsar. The headteacher of the orphanage was a renowned trainer in classical music – Bhai Sain Ditta. Several of Sain Ditta's students served as hazoori raagis at the Darbar Sahib. Some of his famous students included Bhai Taba, Bhai Naseera, Bhai Darshan Singh Komal, and his son, Bhai Desa. Bhai Santa Singh was better than all the rest.

Soon after completing his education at the Yateemkhana, Bhai Santa Singh was employed as a hazoori raagi at the Darbar Sahib during the 1920s. His group included, among others, another famous personality, Bhai Surjan Singh. Both were bestowed with very crisp and melodious voices and could sing in unison. The SGPC had taken control of all the historic Sikh shrines in Punjab and the North-West Frontier Province in 1925. A very high standard of gurmat sangeet was maintained at most gurdwaras, at least during the first three decades after the inception of the SGPC. During those days the Darbar Sahib was known for employing highly accomplished musicians for performing chowkis of shabad kirtan in its sanctum sanctorum. Recommendations by the influential and the powerful were never a factor for recruitment of staff.

Other great musicians in service at the time included the legendry Bhai Lal, Bhai Chand, Bhai Chanan, and Bhai Hira Singh. Before long, with his immense hard work, Bhai Santa Singh had carved a niche for himself. As a first step, he used to grasp the meaning of the shabad to be sung. He modulated his voice to convey the true meaning of the shabad without the need of explaining it through verbal discourse. At times he used to slow down the beat so much that the meaning of each word was understood clearly even by the layman. While reciting the *bir ras bani* (martial hymns) of the Guru Gobind

Singh, he used to convey the atmosphere of battle by increasing the pace of the musical composition.

On special occasions, the Darbar Sahib and Gurdwara Janam Asthan at Nankana Sahib, the two most sacred gurdwaras, used to exchange their leading musicians. Bhai Santa Singh used to go to Nankana Sahib on these occasions.

All India Radio Lahore came into being in 1936, and full-fledged production facilities were added the following year. That was the year when Bhai Santa Singh was also approved as a casual radio artist. During those days, the line-up of the classical vocal radio artists of All India Radio Lahore included, among others, Dalip Chander Vedi, Bade Ghulam Ali Khan, Master Rattan of Phagwara, Master Madan, Dina Qawaal of Jullundur, Mubarik Ali Fateh Ali of Jullundur, and Harish Chander Bali. Leading Sikh religious musicians included Bhai Santa Singh of the Darbar Sahib and Bhai Samund Singh of Nankana Sahib. Malika Pukhraj, Bhai Chhaila of Patiala, Mohammad Rafi, Noorjehan, Zeenat Begum, Shamshad Begum, Dilshad Begum, Mukhtar Begum, Parkash Kaur and Surinder Kaur were considered much junior Punjabi song and ghazal singers.

Occasional singing on All India Radio Lahore increased Bhai Santa Singh's demand. During those days, the Gramaphone Recording Company had opened its modern recording studio in Lahore. Master Ghulam Haider, son of a musician at the Golden Temple, was hired as its music director. He developed a special liking for the voice of Bhai Santa Singh and persuaded him to record some shabads on ten-inch discs. The tunes were either traditional Sikh religious reets handed down from generation to generation or Bhai Santa Singh's own highly melodious creations. The orchestra with special preludes and interludes was, of course, Ghulam Haider's. Eight shabads were recorded on four discs of three minutes each and they became very popular. These recordings were made in 1941-42, but their 45-RPM extended play discs were available till the 1970s. Other Sikh musicians whose recordings of Sikh religious music are among the earliest available on records include Bhai Budh Singh Taan, whose rendering of 'Asa Di Vaar' was available on 12 discs in 78-RPM.

'Asa Di Vaar' by the group of Bhai Sudh Singh Pardhan Singh was also recorded during the 1940s. Similarly, one or two records of shabad gaayan in the voices of Bhai Gurmukh Singh and Sarmukh Singh Fakkar of Nankana Sahib were available in the market. In addition, one disc of shabad gaayan in the voice of the child prodigy, Master Madan, was also recorded during the 1940s. This recording, after disappearing from the market for several decades, is once again available courtesy of some collectors.

Some shabads sung by Bhai Budh Singh Taan and Surinder Kaur were also available. Bhai Samund Singh, though he sang regularly for the radio, did not record his shabad gaayan on gramophone discs until the late 1960s, when, during the quincentennial celebrations of the birth of Guru Nanak, a set of five long-playing records were published.

After the creation of Pakistan in 1947, Bhai Samund Singh also joined Bhai Santa Singh in the service of the Darbar Sahib. They had very different styles of performing shabad kirtan. Bhai Samund Singh used to perform a modified version of the khayal gayaki by leaving the alaap, jorh alaap and the vilambhat lai, as well as the climax dhrutt lai, and instead rendered the entire shabad in madh lai. In contrast, Bhai Santa Singh either sang in the traditional reets handed down from generation to generation or he created his own from the source raagas and raaginis. He used to rehearse the tunes for hours at a stretch to the accompaniment of a tanpura, prior to singing in the gurdwaras.

Bhai Santa Singh lived a simple life. After leaving the service of the Golden Temple he settled in Delhi. In the national capital, he used to ride a bicycle on his way to perform shabad kirtan at Gurdwara Sis Ganj Sahib. He never bargained for money in the gurdwaras he served or the homes of the people. One day an admirer presented a car to him, which he retained for a few days before giving it back. The reason given for spurning the offer was that he used to recite *paath*[51] while cycling and he used to complete the paath during the journey, but when he started being driven in the car, the same distance was travelled in five minutes and he could not complete the paath! Such was the simplicity and lack of greed in Bhai Santa Singh.

Once the famous Bhai Chand was supposed to perform last of all in a special kirtan *diwan*[52] in pre-partition Lahore and Bhai Santa Singh was the penultimate singer. However, Bhai Chand was so impressed with the shabad gaayan by Bhai Santa Singh that he made a request to skip his own turn and asked Bhai Santa Singh to finish the diwan by singing raag *darbari kanra*. Bhai Santa Singh completely mesmerised the audience with his soulful rendition. This story was narrated to me by Bhai Gurdip Singh, the head granthi of New York's Richmond Hill Gurdwara.

As mentioned above, in or about 1949, Bhai Santa Singh abruptly left the service of the SGPC and temporarily moved to New Delhi. Soon after he tried his hand at becoming a building contractor in Assam, but the business did not suit his temperament and carefree lifestyle and he took employment in Gurdwara Sis Ganj Sahib in Old Delhi. Delhi was then fast becoming a city of refugees from West Punjab. Some of his most ardent admirers had moved from Lahore, Gujjranwala, Lyallpur, Montgomery, Sialkot, and

---

[51] Devotional reading or study of Sikh scriptures.

[52] Congregation or assembly.

Sheikhupura. For them, it was a pleasure to listen to his shabad gaayan. On hearing about Bhai Santa Singh's joining the service at Gurdwara Sri Sis Ganj, the crowds at that historic gurdwara started swelling with every passing day.

The refugee sangat of Delhi, especially from the Rawalpindi and Peshawar divisions got so hooked to listening to Bhai Santa Singh's shabad kirtan at Gurdwara Sis Ganj at Chandni Chowk that they insisted that the early morning chowki of 'Asa Di Vaar' must always be performed by his group. The only group allowed to perform the service in the absence of Bhai Santa Singh was the group of Bhai Avtar Singh and Gurcharan Singh and Swaran Singh, formerly of Sultanpur Lodhi in Kapurthala District.

While in Delhi, Bhai Santa Singh became the staff artist of All India Radio Delhi and his live performances of shabad kirtan became a regular feature of its Punjabi program. Some years after 1947, one of the most important members of his group, Bhai Surjan Singh formed his own group. This incident did not go down well with Bhai Santa Singh and he trained his brothers, Bhai Shamsher Singh and Jabarjang Singh, to sing alongside him. This change also did not diminish the popularity of his group. In the meantime, Bhai Surjan Singh's newly created group also became very popular.

To this day the bestselling records of 'Asa Di Vaar' are in the voice of Bhai Surjan Singh.

On the death of India's first Prime Minister, Jawahar Lal Nehru, in 1964, Bhai Santa Singh was the only Sikh religious musician who was specially invited to perform shabad kirtan during the period of mourning at All India Radio Delhi. Some of these recordings are still preserved in the archives of the Delhi station. He was an A-class singer at All India Radio and every class maestro, be it a vocalist or an instrumentalist, had the privilege of being given an opportunity of performing at any of its other stations while visiting. Bhai Santa Singh was one of those elite artists.

All the performances of those artists were supposed to be recorded, yet some were not recorded. Even those whose performances were recorded got destroyed later due to the callousness of the authorities. If all the recordings of Bhai Santa Singh and Bhai Samund Singh would have been preserved, we would have had at least 300 hours of recordings of each! Such musicians are not born every day. It is very unfortunate to have lost their voices.

The late Bhai Harbhajan Singh Yogi was a great admirer of the kirtan shaili of Bhai Santa Singh. In order to train his group in the art of performing shabad gaayan, he wanted to bring one of the students at Bhai Santa Singh's school of music to America. Bibi Amarjit Kaur, who had honed her skills under the guidance of Bhai Santa Singh, was brought to the USA for this purpose. Later she worked in the World Bank and now lives in Northern Virginia, in one of the suburbs of the American Capital. By listening to her, you can get a glimpse of her great mentor. The way she modulates her voice, it appears that she has lived up to the teachings of her mentor.

In 1965, Bhai Santa Singh's former companion, Bhai Surjan Singh suddenly left for his heavenly abode. Although they had parted company years ago, yet Bhai Santa Singh took this loss to heart. For several days he felt very dejected. However, according to the Gurus' message, since life must go on, Bhai Santa Singh did not miss a single kirtan assignment.

A few of Bhai Santa Singh's shabad recital compositions were used in an All India Radio programme produced in 1969 by Professor Harbhajan Singh, a renowned poet, on the 500th birth anniversary of Guru Nanak. According to Dr Madan Gopal Singh, a singer and son of Professor Harbhajan Singh, the recording is in the archives of a private collector, Manjit Bawa, a famous painter, who is no more. He adds that the nearly one-hour long feature broadcast on the national programme of All India Radio was written in Hindi as a tribute to Guru Nanak and was part of the year-long focus to mark the 500th birth anniversary of the Guru. The feature was subsequently published in Punjabi in the form of a booklet by Faqir Singh & Sons, Amritsar.

Some compositions which Madan Gopal Singh distinctly remembers (their melody is permanently etched in his memory and he could reproduce at least the skeletal version) are 'Suni Pukaar Daatar Miti Dhundh', 'Saajan Mainde Rangle', 'Gagan Mai Thal', and 'Jagad Jalanda Rakh Lai'.

He had no idea if Bhai Sahib was specially commissioned (if it was 1969, this couldn't have been possible) to do these recordings or if these were excavated from the AIR archives. In case these recordings were taken from the AIR archives, it does indicate that the AIR has possibly a rich collection of Bhai Sahib's renditions. The bulk of the gurbani rendition in the feature was in the voice of Bhai Santa Singh. There were two other raagis, and if Madan Gopal Singh was not mistaken, these two were by Bhai Avtar Singh and Bhai Amrik Singh. Bhai Sumand Singh was not part of the programme. His rendition of 'Bhujbal Deejai' is part of the archival material that existed on the spool Madan Gopal

Singh had handed over to his painter friend, Manjeet Bawa. Bhai Sahib had come to the main gurdwara in Karol Bagh, New Delhi and had participated in a kirtan darbar that has been attended by many other luminaries as well. The recording was made by Madan Gopal Singh's second cousin and a sound-technician with the AIR, the late Santokh Singh, and subsequently transferred onto the spool. This is where Madan Gopal Singh's narration ends.

Bhai Santa Singh was in great demand all over India for his unique style of shabad kirtan, but he seldom stepped out of Delhi. Once in October 1966, on the persistent request of the knowledgeable sangat of Bombay, he was allowed to go there for a couple of weeks. On hearing this news, the enthusiastic sadh sangat of Bombay was electrified. They had the once-in-a-lifetime experience of listening to Bhai Santa Singh live. They requested more of his time, but the management of Gurdwara Sis Ganj Sahib in Delhi refused to extend his stay because the sangat in Delhi was also missing him and was hooked to listening to his shabad kirtan. Mohammad Rafi, who knew him since their days at All India Radio Lahore, found time every day from his busy recording schedules, to listen to Bhai Sahib's unique voice.

On the day of his departure for Delhi, big crowds gave him a tearful send-off from Bombay. On his way back to Delhi, while on the train, he suffered a massive heart attack. Before medical care could be administered, he had already left for his heavenly abode, at the feet of his divine master, in whose praise he sang every day. Bhai Santa Singh's funeral saw the Sikh community of Delhi in deep mourning. This story was narrated to me by his pupil Bibi Amarjit Kaur.

After Bhai Santa Singh's death, his brother, Bhai Shamsher Singh took over his group. Bhai Shamsher Singh could sing in all the tunes of Bhai Santa Singh, but he lacked the range and modulation. After the death of Bhai Shamsher

Singh about three decades ago, Bhai Santa Singh's nephews, Bhai Harjit Singh and Bhai Gurdip Singh, have taken over the baton and they are keeping his tradition alive. They cannot match the dexterity of Bhai Santa Singh, but they have kept all his reets alive.

Today they are the leading musicians of the Delhi Sikh Gurdwara Management Committee (DSGMC) and are held in high esteem. However, due to old age, even they are not performing shabad kirtan with the same regularity that they used to.

Bhai Mangal Singh, another disciple of Bhai Santa Singh, also kept his style alive for a few years. After his death, his brilliant son, Bhai Manohar Singh is now the torchbearer of the kirtan style of Bhai Santa Singh.

Bhai Manohar Singh

(Courtesy: APNA. Edited for sikhchic.com 13 July 2012)

5

Bhai Piara Singh

A Link with Pakistani Punjab

Bhai Piara Singh was born in an agricultural family of Chakk No. 296 of Gojra Mandi Tehsil of district Lyallpur in Multan division of undivided Punjab. According to his son, Bhai Jaswant Singh, his father was born around 1918. However, there is no available record of his birth. Bhai Piara Singh's father was Punjab Singh and his mother's name was Aas Kaur. He was the eldest among his brothers.

Since childhood, Piara Singh loved music. He was especially interested in Sikh religious music, and he had a desire to learn shabad kirtan. Someone guided him to visit the Dera of Sant Baba Nand Singh (famous as Sant Kaleranwale). In Baba Nand Singh's Dera, he met a maverick musician known as Bhai Sujan Singh. He had a strong classical base and he used to sing shabads in the qawwali and ghazal styles. Young Piara Singh got fascinated with this uncommon style and expressed his desire to learn music from him.

Bhai Sujan Singh wanted to hear Piara Singh sing whatever he could. The latter sang an old Punjabi folk song 'Vanjhli Walia Morh Muharan'. Bhai Sujan Singh did not disapprove of his style and voice. After persistent visitations, Bhai Sujan Singh, later called Sant Sujan Singh, started teaching intricacies of classical music to him. Piara Singh was a quick learner. He started learning the shabads and also learnt the basics of the various raagas.

Bhai Piara Singh put together a rag-tag raagi jatha consisting of his younger brother, Kirpal Singh and a budding musician from his village, Gurmukh Singh, who became the tabla player. They started performing shabad kirtan in the village and the cluster of hamlets around it.

In search of greener pastures, he moved to Lahore around 1940, where he took a job in Gurdwara Sri Dera Sahib. Although the gurdwara had access to a number of rababi Muslim musicians, they had a brilliant secretary in Giani Mohinder Singh, who later on became the longest-serving secretary of the SGPC in Amritsar. On persistent public demand, he got Bhai Piara Singh appointed as the head hazoori raagi of Gurdwara Dera Sahib Lahore.

Out of curiosity or maybe due to a burning desire to become a radio artist, Bhai Piara Singh showed up at the studios of All India Radio Lahore. Surprisingly, he was selected as a radio artist, and he started doing shabad kirtan approximately once a month at All India Radio Lahore. This arrangement continued up to August of 1947. He was doing 'Asa Di Vaar' and other chowkis at the historic gurdwaras.

One day, while Bhai Piara Singh was performing shabad kirtan at the radio station, suddenly serious rioting erupted. Under the instructions of senior officials of All India Radio, he was escorted out of the radio station by security officials. His youngest son, Harbhajan Singh, was badly scared leading to a bad bout of an upset stomach as well. Somehow the family managed to move out of Lahore and they crossed the Wagha border into India.

After a brief stay in Amritsar, they were moved to a refugee camp in Ludhiana. His son, Jaswant Singh, recovered from the shock, but the younger one, Harbhajan Singh, passed away.

This family was allotted some land in village Khizrabad in the Karnal district. Prior to that, they stayed, for some time, in Rahon town of the Doaba region. They kept performing shabad kirtan in the villages of Nawanshehar and Garh Shanker Tehsils in Doaba. However, their stay in the Doaba region was at best a stopgap arrangement as Bhai Piara Singh wanted to relocate to some other place, where his talents could be better appreciated.

Destiny brought them to Patiala where Bhai Piara Singh approached the management of Gurdwara Sri Dukh Niwaran Sahib. The secretary of the Sikh Dharam Pracharak Board was Giani Mohinder Singh, and their President General was Gurdial Singh Harika. They liked his voice and thus accommodated him on the staff of the gurdwara.

In 1960, since Bhai Piara Singh became unhappy with the other members of his raagi jatha, he asked his son, Jaswant Singh, who had quite a melodious voice, to join the jatha. Jaswant Singh was serving in the Electricity Department of Pepsu at Nabha. Since his first love was Sikh religious music, he resigned from the government job and joined his father's raagi jatha. Bhai Piara Singh's sweet and melodious voice, by then, had made the jatha quite popular in Patiala and the neighbouring areas of Ambala, Chandigarh, Sarhind, Nabha, and Sangrur.

In December of 1962, the entire top leadership of the Shiromani Akali Dal (SAD) and the SGPC went to Patna Sahib to celebrate the birth anniversary of Sri Guru Gobind

Singh ji. This included Sant Fateh Singh, President of SAD, Sant Channan Singh, President of the SGPC, Giani Chet Singh, the most influential high priest of the Golden Temple, and Giani Mohinder Singh, Secretary of the SGPC. Giani Mohinder Singh had informed his seniors about the qualities and skills of Bhai Piara Singh, who had, by then, become a famous kirtania. On 31st January 1963, he was transferred to the Golden Temple, a highly coveted place of posting.

Among his duties was the performance of 'Asa Di Vaar'. His stay at the Golden Temple proved very fruitful. He was invited to perform shabad kirtan in most of the large gurdwaras in the major cities of India. He was also asked by the Polydor Recording Company of Germany to record 'Asa Di Vaar' for commercial distribution all over India. The knowledgeable listeners of gurmat sangeet rate his rendition of 'Asa Di Vaar' better than the best-selling 'Asa Di Vaar' sung by Bhai Surjan Singh.

Bhai Piara Singh recorded his music on discs on the 500th birth anniversary of Sri Guru Nanak Dev ji in 1969. His sons, Bhai Jaswant Singh, Bhai Jagtar Singh, and Bhai Manjeet Singh served his raagi jatha from time to time. He had two other sons – Bhai Jagdeep Singh and Bhai Satbir Singh. He had only one daughter – Paramjit Kaur. Bhai Piara Singh served the Golden Temple up to the end of 1969 and then returned to his home base in Patiala.

One of the wealthiest Sikh industrialists of that time was Sardar Sewa Singh, the owner of Sardar Foundry in Batala. He was one of the most ardent admirers of Bhai Piara Singh. Whenever Bhai Piara Singh needed money, he invariably came to his rescue.

Towards the end of his life, Bhai Piara Singh had settled down in Patiala. The people of Chandigarh too loved his style of kirtan. He performed kirtan several times at the Sector 19 Gurdwara. He performed shabad kirtan in

Chandigarh on 6th March 1988, one of his most memorable performances. After that, when he complained of uneasiness, he was taken to Patiala and was admitted to Rajindra Hospital, where he breathed his last on 7th March 1988.

One of his tunes for the shabad 'Prabh Dori Haath Tumhare' has become immortal. Several raagis after him have been heard performing the same shabad in the same tune. Now his sons, too, are following in his footsteps as kirtanias. Bhai Piara Singh is no more with us, but his voice will remain with us forever in the form of records, cassette tapes, CDs, and pen drives.

6

Bhai Avtar Singh and Gurcharan Singh

The Old Guards of Dhrupad-based Gurmat Sangeet

Bhai Avtar Singh and Bhai Gurcharan Singh, formerly of village Saidpur near the holy town of Sultanpur Lodhi in erstwhile Kapurthala State (presently Kapurthala district of Punjab) are considered a live wire between the music of the era of the great ten Gurus and the modern-day Sikh community and the world. Worthy sons of Bhai Jwala Singh ji, they started learning vintage gurmat sangeet from their iconic father. All the meticulous training they received from him reflects in their style and substance.

Bhai Gurcharan Singh, the elder son, was born in 1915 and at the young age of six or eight years, he was initiated into rigorous training in classical music. By the age of ten, he was inducted into his father's kirtan jatha as a tabla player. At the same time, he was made to cram up as much Gurbani as possible. Later on, Bhai Gurcharan Singh learnt several other instruments, including the taus and the suranda. He switched to playing the harmonium around 1936.

Bhai Avtar Singh was born in 1925. Even he was inducted into his father's jatha around 1936, and for the next 12 years, both brothers were an integral part of the jatha of their father.

Bhai Jwala Singh and his sons are acknowledged to be true dhrupadias while most of the other stalwarts are called khayali-style gayaks. Bhai Avtar Singh and Bhai Gurcharan Singh vehemently asserted all their life that the original gurmat sangeet and the kirtan chowkis prevalent during the time of the ten Sikh Gurus were based on the dhrupad and dhamar format.

For me, there is no reason to question the wisdom and research of Bhai Avtar Singh and Bhai Gurcharan Singh. Even Late Bhai Samund Singh ji often agreed with this claim. My father was of the view that the khayal format of North Indian classical music started taking shape only during the lifetime of the tenth master of the Sikh faith, Guru Gobind Singh ji. Bhai Balbir Singh, a former hazoori raagi of the Golden Temple Amritsar, an ustad Sikh musician and former *Shiromani Raagi*[53] also confirms this view. If we go by the baani enshrined in the Sri Guru Granth Sahib ji, most of it was composed by the first five Gurus with a small portion added from the baani that was composed by the ninth Guru. As such the originally-sung Sikh music was, of course, composed to be sung in the Dhrupad style of classical music.

Considering all this, the music often rendered by Bhai Jwala Singh ji and his brilliant sons was indeed the original

[53] Chief musician.

form of Sikh religious music. For the Sikh community, it is important to keep this stream of music alive today. Bhai Avtar Singh and Gurcharan Singh have claimed that one of their ancestors (some 11 to 16 generations ago) had been regularly present, and participating, in the diwans that were held in the presence of Sri Guru Gobind Singh ji. According to them, their ancestor had learnt the music of the Guru's darbar especially from the rababi musicians of the times. This music was essentially in the dhrupad, dhamaar and the partal formats.

After Guru Gobind Singh ji left Anandpur Sahib for the South of India (Sri Huzoor Sahib Nanded in Maharashtra), Bhai Jwala Singh's ancestor returned to his family home in Saidpur near Sultanpur Lodhi, where he kept this unique and valuable musical tradition alive by imparting training to the coming generations within the family and thus also keeping them tied to the not-so lucrative profession of a kirtania. Roughly, during the same time, some other musicians at Tarn Taran and Kapurthala were also performing shabad kirtan in the dhrupad and dhamar style, but they somehow missed the limelight. With the passage of time, the dhrupadias of places other than Sultanpur Lodhi vanished from the scene, or they shifted to the more common khayal style.

After separating from their father's umbrella, the raagi jatha continued doing several Shabad kirtan programmes on their own. Around 1948-1949, Bhai Gurcharan Singh and Bhai Avtar Singh's group applied for and received approval from All India Radio Jalandhar, Amritsar as B-grade casual artists. This gave them both name and fame and the radio listeners started liking their renditions. Within the next two years, they moved to Delhi and got employment as hazoori raagis at the Gurdwara Sis Ganj Sahib in Chandni Chowk in Old Delhi. In seniority, and next only to Bhai Santa Singh ji,

Bhai Gurcharan Singh on the left and
Bhai Avtar Singh on the right

their jatha received their due acclamation from the lovers of gurmat sangeet not only in Delhi but in Punjab and the neighbouring states too. While performing shabad gayan in old tunes at All India Radio Delhi, Bhai Gurcharan Singh mostly played the tanpura instead of harmonium and, for some time, he was the lead singer in the group. After a few years, Bhai Gurcharan Singh bestowed the honour of the lead singer, known as the *jathedar*, on his younger brother, Bhai Avtar Singh. After the year 2000, Bhai Avtar Singh switched to playing the taus, and he received acclaim for that.

Gurdwara Bridgewater in Somerset County of New Jersey, USA has a special relationship with the raagi jatha of Bhai Avtar Singh Gurcharan Singh. They visited the United States for the first time in 1979, the year during which the building of the oldest gurdwara of New Jersey was purchased. After that, they have been visiting the USA once every three years and every time, they have performed shabad kirtan at Gurdwara Bridgewater. Once during the 1980s, the management of Gurdwara Richmond Hill, New York, sponsored the visit of the raagi jatha of Bhai Dilbagh Singh Gulbagh Singh. During the same year, Gurdwara Bridgewater sponsored the visit of Bhai Avtar Singh and Gurcharan Singh too. Sardar Pargat Singh, himself an accomplished musician and a student of a great maestro Master Rattan of Phagwara, was the general secretary of Gurdwara Richmond Hill. Sardar Pargat Singh wanted to hold a kirtan darbar, where both great jathas would perform kirtan. It was finally decided to hold this at Gurdwara Bridgewater and Sardar Pargat Singh was also invited to perform kirtan.

The programme started at 7 p.m. and ended well past midnight. When Bhai Gulbagh Singh performed a difficult taan, Bhai Gurcharan Singh applauded. Similarly, when Bhai Avtar Singh and Gurcharan Singh started a partal in raag Darbari Kanrha, Bhai Dilbagh Singh gave compliments. Sardar Pargat Singh came with his musician daughters and sons. They had tanpuras in their hands. They not only used the tanpura for their own accompaniment, but they gave company to the jathas of Bhai Dilbagh Singh, Gulbagh Singh, and Bhai Avtar Singh-Gurcharan Singh as well. It was a memorable evening of Sikh devotional music.

Although Bhai Avtar Singh had been bestowed with the award of Shiromani Raagi during the 1980s, his elder brother, Bhai Gurcharan Singh, got it later, only in 2008.

Bhai Avtar Singh, the younger of the two brothers, left for his heavenly abode after a brief bout with cancer, on 23rd November 2006. Throughout his life as a kirtania he remembered all the 500 reets and had recorded all of them for the Punjabi University Patiala. He has also recorded approximately 380 of these reets for T-Series Recording Company for a commercial release.

The void that Bhai Avtar Singh has left in the field of gurmat sangeet is rather difficult to fill. We will all miss him. On the day of his funeral thousands of mourners, including those families where he had performed kirtan on happy and sad occasions, came to see him. Bhai Avtar Singh was a very sweet and friendly individual, who always greeted people with a broad smile. He may have gone, but his memories will linger forever. His legacy is still alive. His brilliant son, Bhai Kultar Singh, accompanied by his cousin, Bhai Swaran Singh, is keeping the unique ancient tradition alive. May God bless them with talent, good health, and fortitude.

Bhai Swaran Singh

After about a decade the brother duo was joined by their nephew, Bhai Swaran Singh, who used to play the tabla. Bhai Gurcharan Singh was responsible for training his nephew in the art of playing the tabla in most of the taals used by the Sikh religious musicians. Whatever Bhai Swaran Singh learnt from Bhai Gurcharan Singh, he used to rehearse for hours every day. This trio served the historic Sikh shrines of

Delhi for almost half a century. During this period, they received several state and national honours including that of Shiromani Kirtania from the Languages Department of the Punjab Government.

Bhai Baldeep Singh

One of the nephews of Bhai Avtar Singh and Bhai Gurcharan Singh is Bhai Baldeep Singh. He is an accomplished tabla player and he sings most of the reets of the family quite well. In addition, he is a historian in his own right. Several times Bhai Baldeep Singh has accompanied his uncles in performing shabad kirtan. Once in Gurdwara Bridgewater, he accompanied Bhai Avtar Singh and his group where he played the tabla. It was also another memorable event.

Bhai Kultar Singh

Around 1995, Bhai Gurcharan Singh took retirement from the jatha and in the new millennium, Bhai Avtar Singh's younger son, Bhai Kultar Singh, an engineer by profession, joined the jatha. After forming a new raagi jatha with the inclusion of Bhai Kultar Singh, Bhai Avtar Singh quickly started imparting the family's ancestral education in Sikh music to his technocrat-turned-musician son. Bhai Kultar Singh was still midway in the learning process when Bhai Avtar Singh left for his heavenly abode at the feet of the Guru. More about Bhai Kultar Singh in the next chapter.

7

Bhai Kultar Singh

A Livewire Between the New Generation and the Music of the Era of the Ten Sikh Gurus

Being the grandson of the illustrious Bhai Jwala Singh ji who was blessed by a 14-year long stay by Sri Guru Nanak Dev ji in Sultanpur Lodhi, and being the son of the highly celebrated Bhai Avtar Singh ji, the former hazoori raagi of Gurdwara Sis Ganj Sahib of Old Delhi, Bhai Kultar Singh has several advantages to his credit as a Gurbani kirtania. His ancestors were associated with the Guru darbars around 400 years ago. As such, they had a unique exposure to the prevalent traditions of gurbani kirtan in the Guru darbars. One of his predecessors, 14–15 generations ago, had had the unique privilege of serving in the Guru darbar of the tenth master, Sri Guru Guru Gobind Singh ji, as one of the several kirtanias, while the Guru was in Punjab.

After the period of the great Gurus, Bhai Kultar Singh's ancestors started living permanently in the village of Fateabad in the Amritsar district and later shifted to village Saidpur near Sultanpur Lodhi in erstwhile Kapurthala state.

In addition to the daily chores of performing shabad kirtan, the family did farming as well. According to Late Bhai Avtar Singh, his predecessors kept alive the ancient gurmat kirtan traditions of the Guru darbars, in their pristine purity within the family. These lofty traditions, although getting extinct now in other gharanas, are still alive within this family.

Some of the hallmarks of the ancient gurmat sangeet traditions include renditions of the shabads in the Dhrupad and Dhamar formats. Panjtall Aswari, Chartall, Soolphag and several other rare taals prevalent in the Guru darbars are preserved within the kirtan shaili of this family. The partal tradition too, while dying elsewhere, is alive with Bhai Kultar Singh's group.

My late father once told me that the biggest fountain head shrines of gurmat sangeet during the past two centuries have been the Golden Temple in Amritsar and the Gurdwara Janam Asthan Sri Nankana Sahib. Both these shrines are located within 50 miles of Punjab's capital and its cultural centre of Lahore. Because of this, all the innovations in fine arts that occurred in Lahore and the other centres of music elsewhere in India, found their way into Amritsar and Nankana Sahib. Thus, the kirtan traditions at Amritsar and Nankana Sahib kept changing during the past two centuries. In the present day, the most popular khayal format of North Indian classical music, which was in its infancy during the period of Sri Guru Gobind Singh ji, developed extensively. Lahore became the harbinger of the evolutions of new traditions of classical music. The family of Bhai Jwala Singh lived in far-away Sultanpur Lodhi, which is located away from the much-travelled Grand Trunk Road. Due to the remoteness of the location, this family maintained its traditions of music.

Bhai Avtar Singh inherited 500 ancient tunes of gurmat sangeet from his father, Bhai Jwala Singh, and Bhai Kultar, an engineer by profession, after switching to the rendition of gurmat sangeet, has learnt at least 400 tunes based on all 31 raagas included in the Sri Guru Granth Sahib ji. Bhai Kultar Singh's voice is a rich male voice which he modulates effortlessly for all the reets that he performs in.

In addition, Bhai Kultar Singh enjoys a very conspicuous command of the English language. He has grasped the meanings of the shabads rather well and he can explain its meaning to the new generation very effectively in English. His command over the language is helping Sikh families living in Europe, America and Canada understand the meaning of the shabads better. The congregations of old and new generations in the gurdwaras in North America have liked his kirtan shaili. The newer generation has liked his *viakhia*[54], or interpretation, of the Guru's word enshrined in the holy Sri Guru Granth Sahib.

Bhai Avtar Singh left for his heavenly abode on 23rd November 2006.

Bhai Swaran Singh, Bhai Avtar Singh's nephew, had been the tabla player of the original jatha consisting of Bhai Jwala Singh for five years, from 1947 to Bhai Jwala Singh's demise in 1952. After the death of Bhai Jwala Singh, Bhai Avtar Singh led the jatha, assisted by Bhai Gurcharan Singh and Bhai Swarn Singh, who was the tabla accompaniment since the 1950s, and is now a member of the jatha led by Bhai Kultar Singh. The advantage of Bhai Swaran Singh's presence in the group is that he can play all the taals, which have been played by the Sikh religious musicians since the times of the great Gurus. He also remembers most of the shabads included in the holy book, Sri Guru Granth Sahib ji, by heart, and knows most of the tunes handed down from generation to generation within this family of musicians. His voice is also very good and matches well with that of Bhai

---

[54] Elaboration or discourse.

Kultar Singh. The third member of the group used to be Bhai Manmohan Singh. He is a descendent of a Kashmiri family of traditional Sikh priests and religious musicians. His voice quality is also great. The three musicians together make a good team. However, according to my information, the third member keeps changing.

Bhai Kultar Singh

8

Bhai Bakhshish Singh

A Genius

Since the time of the great Gurus, Amritsar has produced great icons of music including the Gurus themselves. Amritsar in 1904 also produced a great thumri singer, Indu Bala, whose influence is obvious on some Sikh religious musicians of the yore, including the legendary Bhai Samund Singh of Gurdwara Janam Asthan Sri Nankana Sahib in Pakistan. Some other musicians of Nankana Sahib, like Bhai Gurmukh Singh, Sarmukh Singh Fakkar, Bhai Pal Singh, and Bhai Jaswant Singh were also influenced by her. Bhai Agha Faiz, a famous folk and shabad singer was also a product of Amritsar. He was a very soft mannered and sophisticated musician. Amritsar also produced two great female ghazal singers, Mukhtar Begum and more recently Farida Khanum. It was home to the reputed female classical singer, Zahida Parveen as well. Amritsar is also credited with producing one of India's earliest music directors, Master Ghulam Haider. He was the son of a musician of Sri Darbar Sahib. Pakistan's great playback singer, Zubaida Khanum (active years 1950 to 1960) was a daughter of Amritsar too. In 1924, rural Amritsar gave birth to India's longest-reigning and the most celebrated film playback singer Mohammad

Rafi, who ruled India's male film (Hindi/Urdu) playback singing from 1947 to his death in 1980. Amritsar was the birthplace of Daleep Vedi too. In more recent history, the city produced the likes of Bhai Lal Senior, a descendant of Bhai Abdullah and Bhai Nath Mal of Sri Guru Teg Bahadur's time, Bhai Nasira, a descendent of Bhai Satta and Bhai Balwand (court musicians of the fourth and the fifth Guru), and Bhai Chand Senior.

In 1933, two more icons of Sikh religious music were born in Amritsar. They were Bhai Bakhshish Singh of village Makhanwindi and Bhai Balbir Singh of Tarn Taran. Bhai Bakhshish Singh was the son of another well-known Sikh religious musician, Bhai Kirpal Singh, who served all his life in Sri Darbar Sahib at Tarn Taran. Bhai Kirpal Singh was the son Bhai Jawala Singh[55], another great Sikh religious musician.

The town of Tarn Taran was a great centre of music, supplying a steady stream of musicians to the Golden Temple. In turn, Tarn Taran was fed by some other gurdwaras in its vicinity like Khadoor Sahib (its rababi musicians were called *khadoorias*), Goindwal Sahib, Sultanpur Lodhi and Kapurthala. Of course, Bhai Jawala Singh of Tarn Taran must have learnt a lot from the rababi Muslim kirtanias of Tarn Taran and its vicinity. There is no doubt that he passed on his education to his son.

Bhai Bakhshish Singh in childhood stayed with his father in Tarn Taran. He inherited gurmat sangeet from him and his grandfather. Since gurbani was in the family, he started learning shabads of the Sri Guru Granth Sahib ji from the young age of three.

---

[55] Bhai Jawala Singh of Tarn Taran: We should not confuse Bhai Jawala Singh of Tarn Taran with Bhai Jwala Singh of village Saidpur, near Sultanpur Lodhi in erstwhile Kapurthala State.

There was a gurmat sangeet *vidyalaya*[56] headed by a great teacher, Bhai Puran Singh in Tarn Taran. Bhai Balbir Singh received his training from this institution too. In addition to receiving training from his father and grandfather, Bhai Bakhshish Singh also enrolled himself in this highly acclaimed school. This great vidyalaya had mastered a lot of ancient kirtan reets of the rababi musicians, in addition to the treasure of gursikh musicians. Obviously, Bakhshish Singh learnt a lot from this seminary. Bhai Puran Singh himself used to sing on very high notes, using his immense lung power. This proficiency Bhai Bakhshish imbibed from Bhai Puran Singh. All his life Bhai Puran Singh used to riyaz for hours every day and he expected the same from his proteges too. Due to his dedication, Bhai Bakhshish Singh became a favourite trainee musician of Bhai Puran Singh.

By the time he was five to six years old, this frail-looking child insisted on accompanying his father when he used to sing 'Asa Di Vaar' at Gurdwara Sri Darbar Sahib in Tarn Taran. A curious child is usually a great learner, and by constantly watching his father singing 'Asa Di Vaar' almost daily, Bakhshish Singh learnt all the *chhakkas*[57] by heart.

One day he could not resist the temptation of reciting the chhakkas of the 'Asa Di Vaar' alongside his father.

His voice was very shrill, almost feminine, and he could go to the highest notes without straining his vocal cords. His father initially hesitated to include his son in the group, but later, realising that his son was perfectly in sur and taal, he accepted young Bakhshish Singh's entry into his group of musicians. This also encouraged him to teach his son some commonly used shabads of gurbani and he imparted education about some of the ragaas as well. On some occasions, Bakhshish Singh assisted his grandfather too.

---

[56] An educational institution.

[57] Stanzas of six lines each.

The rural peasantry of Tarn Taran – Patti and the Khadoor Sahib belt of those days – had a good ear for music. Some of them fell in love with Bakhshish Singh's voice. With love and affection, many of his rural admirers lifted him up and repeatedly cheered for him after the kirtan was over. Each time he was seen resetting his ruffled turban.

Before attaining the age of ten he had learnt to play both the tabla and the harmonium. He was familiar with most of the taals too. Learning gurbani continued simultaneously. Approximately by the age of 12, he became a full-fledged kirtania. Young Bakhshish Singh became so popular that people insisted on his inclusion in the all-adult jatha of Bhai Kirpal Singh. During those days, Tarn Taran had become the third biggest centre of Sikh religious music. Both Gurdwara Dera Sahib in Lahore and the Golden Temple in Amritsar recruited their best musicians from Tarn Taran.

Pakistan was created in 1947 and the province of Punjab was bifurcated. Both Ambala and Jalandhar divisions became a part of India while Rawalpindi and Multan divisions became a part of Pakistan. The central Lahore division had to be bifurcated. Lahore, Sialkot, Sheikhupura (including Nankana Sahib, the birthplace of Sri Guru Nanak Dev ji), and Gujranwala were allocated to Pakistan while Amritsar and Gurdaspur were given to India. Tarn Taran was a Sikh majority *tehsil*. During rioting, the Sikhs clearly had the upper hand in Tarn Taran. The Muslims (including the rababi Muslim musicians) were forcibly uprooted from Tarn Taran hence. Bhai Bakhshish Singh was only 14-years-old then. This chain of events might have influenced his psyche. It is possible that he became more profound after seeing the barbarity. He had always been very secular in his views and yearned to listen to the leading Muslim musicians like Bade Ghulam Ali Khan, Nazaqat Ali Khan, Salamat Ali Khan, Amanat Ali Khan, Fateh Ali Khan, and Mubarik Ali Khan-

Fateh Ali Khan qawwals. At times he even listened to Malika-e-Mausiqui Roshan Ara Begum, Begum Akhtar, and Shobha Gurtu too. Among the Sikhs, he was a great fan of Bhai Samund Singh and Bhai Santa Singh. He even listened to Sant Sujan Singh of New Delhi quite regularly.

Bhai Bakhshish Singh got married in 1952 when he was not even 20 years old. He received his degree of gyani from Panjab University in Solan in 1954. After that, he became a radio artist of All India Radio, Jalandhar. Initially, he got the B-class category. Becoming a radio artist teaches the importance of time. At the radio stations, one must complete a shabad within a stipulated time frame. Bhai Samund Singh was an expert in finishing the complete shabad in nine and a half minutes, seven minutes, and four and a half minutes. Bhai Bakhshish Singh also mastered this discipline very quickly. Most of the raagis used to stretch a shabad too long and they supplemented the shabad with katha too, but Bhai Bakhshish Singh seldom performed katha. Sardar Jodh Singh, the second in order of seniority at All India Radio, Jalandhar, was a great admirer and guide of Bhai Bakhshish Singh. He used his vast experience to get the best out of Bhai Bakhshish Singh.

From 1951, Bhai Bakhshish Singh's raagi jatha served in Tarn Taran as employees of the SGPC for nearly a decade. After that, there were three short-duration postings in Gurdwara Baba Bakala (in Amritsar district), Anandpur Sahib (in the then Hoshiarpur district), and Muktsar (in the then Ferozepore district). He was always in great demand elsewhere too.

Around 1965, Bhai Bakhshish was posted by the SGPC in Gurdwara Dukh Niwaran Sahib at Patiala, where he performed duties for about a decade. During his stay there, he served as a guest musician at Gurdwara Bahadurgarh Sahib on Rajpura Road and Gurdwara Fatehgarh Sahib in

Sirhind. The sangat of Chandigarh and Ambala also became a great admirer of his sweet and versatile voice. While posted at Patiala, he was assisted by another brilliant musician, Dr Jagir Singh, for three years from 1967 to 1969. That was the period when his voice was extensively recorded by All India Radio Jalandhar and his recordings were broadcast by All India Radio stations in Delhi, Simla, Lucknow, Jaipur and even in Radio Kashmir Srinagar and Jammu.

The biggest event in his life was the 500th birth anniversary of Sri Guru Nanak Dev ji in 1969. Both Bhai Surjan Singh and Bhai Santa Singh died in 1966 and Bhai Samund Singh was getting old. Bhai Bakhshish Singh was in the prime of his youth then. Hence, during the 500th *parkash purb*[58] celebration, he took the centre stage. Many records were cut in his unique high-pitched voice. All India Radio, Jalandhar conferred on him the coveted status of an A-class artist after this programme.

[58] Anniversary.

One of the specialities of Bhai Bakhshish Singh was his rendition of the baani of the tenth master, Sri Guru Gobind Singh ji, in the highest notes. He used to render the 'Bir Rus Baani' of Sri Guru Gobind Singh ji in his God-gifted high-pitched but melodious voice. Some of the *nihang singhs* (known affectionately as the Tenth Guru's beloved army), loved to throng to the gurdwaras where he used to sing. Though he hailed from Amritsar district, Bhai Bakhshish Singh loved his tenure at Patiala. During his tenure, there were other highly professional musicians like Bhai Joginder Singh and Mohinder Singh formerly of Nankana Sahib, but Bhai Bakhshish Singh had created a special place for himself.

He was known for speaking each word of gurbani clearly. This made the interpretation of each word easy. After Dr Jagir Singh parted company with Bhai Bakhshish Singh, he had to pick other musicians, many times randomly. At this stage, Surjit Singh of Sangrur district joined him as a vocal accompaniment. Surjit Singh was not an expert in classical music, but as far as the reets (applied classical and folk music) were concerned, he was very quick in grasping the tunes. Surjit Singh stayed with him for ten years, including his stay at the Golden Temple of Amritsar. One of the most favourite reets of the olden days was used by him in the rendition of shabad: 'Paati torheh Maalini'. No other raagi could match his unique manner of rendition of this shabad.

Once Bhai Bakhshish Singh was requested to sing 'Asa Di Vaar' by India's biggest music company, the His Master's Voice Recording Company of Calcutta. The offer was very lucrative. He approached Dr Jagir Singh to sing along with him. Somehow the proposal did not materialise, otherwise, we would have had another bestseller rendition of 'Asa Di Vaar', in addition to Bhai Surjan Singh's landmark rendition issued on two LP records.

In 1975, the tercentennial anniversary of the martyrdom of Guru Teg Bahadur ji, was observed all over India. By then Bhai Samund Singh had also died. Bhai Bakhshish Singh was the leading musician at that time. Some records in his voice were published, which became very popular.

Bhai Bakhshish Singh earned a lot of fame but had an unfulfilled desire to serve the Golden Temple (Sach Khand Sri Darbar Sahib) in Amritsar. Being one of the senior-most and popular musicians employed by the SGPC, it was not difficult for him to get a posting at the Golden Temple. The then President of the SGPC, Jathedar Gurcharan Singh Tohra, was known to be a tough administrator. Bhai Bakhshish Singh's request to him was accepted. The other senior raagis at the Golden Temple at that time were Bhai Balbir Singh of Tarn Taran, Bhai Hari Singh, and Bhai Piara Singh. Bhai Principal Baldev Singh joined later.

From 1975 to 1980, for more than five years, Bhai Bakhshish Singh rendered his services at the Golden Temple which had several advantages. His side companion was Bhai Surjit Singh, who also gained in stature.

While in Amritsar, he often visited All India Radio in Jalandhar to perform live and for archiving of his music for future. In 1978, on Baisakhi Day, Amritsar saw its first large scale clash between the Sikhs and the Nirankaris. Peace in Amritsar was shattered. The tension it generated lasted a long time. The situation worsened in 1980.

Meanwhile some differences of opinion occurred between the SGPC and Bhai Bakhshish Singh. This resulted in his resignation after a long tenure with the SGPC. He left Amritsar and became a freelance musician. Rather than staying put in the most influential, but otherwise turbulent Sikh city of Amritsar, an apolitical Bhai Bakhshish Singh returned to the quiet small-town life of Patiala for a low profile but peaceful life. His love for good classical music never diminished. Whenever he had time, he listened to the great masters of classical music.

The style of shabad kirtan evolved by Bhai Bakhshish Singh had become very popular among the Sikh elite. The demand for his kirtan came from all over India. New Delhi and Chandigarh saw a huge surge for it, while the same was true about Bombay and Calcutta too. During his quieter years, Bhai Bakhshish Singh made it possible to get the finest education for his children. This was even though he was never financially very comfortable and, at best, lived from hand to mouth.

His long-time assistant-musician, Surjit Singh, who stayed back in the service of the SGPC in Amritsar, was politically very shrewd. On his relentless insistence, he was allowed to form his raagi jatha, which stayed in Amritsar for another five years or so and then he obtained a visa for the United States of America.

During the intervening period, the SGPC lost its grip over the administration of the historic Sikh shrines. Then operation Blue Star occurred in Sri Darbar Sahib, which spelled the economic doom of this industrial and commercial hub of Punjab.

During the mid-1980s and later years, Bhai Bakhshish Singh had no proper raagi jatha. Those who invited him to their functions, did so on the strength of his voice. His once very popular raagi jatha used to be improvised by arranging musicians mostly by the host families.

Punjab was passing through a period of insurgency during the 1980s and early 1990s. During this period, a lot of bloodshed occurred all over the state. Many innocent people were killed in cold blood. On an ill-fated day Bhai Bakhshish Singh was also hit by bullets. He was then in Chandigarh to perform shabad kirtan at a private residence, when all of a sudden, the assailants struck.[59] Later on, his assassins realised, what they had done. They made attempts to apologise to the bereaved family for their hasty action, but I must quote an old English adage: 'Those who live by the sword, die by the sword'. His assassins were also eliminated in as much cold blood by the police. Two blunders don't make one right and bullets once fired cannot be recalled. The Sikh community had lost a great musician at the young age of 57, when he could have served the community for at least two more decades. Yes, Bhai Bakhshish Singh is no more with us, but his music and voice shall remain alive forever.

---

[59] Two other incidents of similar nature had occurred earlier too. A senior musician, Bhai Amrik Singh of the Golden Temple, was killed while performing his duty at the Golden Temple in June 1984 during Operation Blue Star. He was killed by a stray army bullet. Another assassination occurred, when another popular Sikh religious musician, Bhai Davinder Singh of Gurdaspur, was killed in a similar fashion during the peak of insurgency in Punjab.

9

Bhai Balbir Singh

The Man Who Never Got his Due

There are only two families of Sikh religious musicians, who claim to have been blessed by the great Gurus to perform gurmat sangeet in accordance with the specific instructions issued by the great Gurus themselves. The first family consists of the sons (Bhai Gurcharan Singh and Bhai Avtar Singh) and a grandson (Bhai Kultar Singh) of Bhai Jwala Singh (1872–1952) of the village Saidpur in the Sultanpur Lodhi tehsil of district Kapurthala. They claim that their style of gurmat sangeet is based on the Dhrupad and Dhamar variety of North Indian classical music, which was prevalent during the times of all ten Gurus.

The other family is of Bhai Balbir Singh, formerly of Tarn Taran and later of Sri Darbar Sahib in Amritsar, who claim to have been especially blessed by the fifth master, Sri Guru Arjan Dev ji, to perform shabad kirtan to fill the vacuum left by the refusal of Bhai Satta and Bhai Balwand. The leading rababi Muslim musicians of the time, when in anger at not being compensated adequately by the Fifth Guru, they walked out, leaving every devout Sikh flabbergasted. I have no reason for not agreeing with the contentions of both these families of learned musicians because their music certainly traces back its origin to the dhrupad, dhamar and partal based music that was prevalent at the times of the great Gurus. Several recordings of both families are available.

I can add a third family to this list too. It is of Late Bhai Santa Singh, originally of Sri Darbar Sahib in Amritsar and later of Gurdwara Sri Sis Ganj Sahib in Old Delhi. His style of gurmat sangeet had a marked similarity with the pattern of music followed by the other two musical dynasties. The famous musicians of Gurdwara Janam Asthan Sri Nankana Sahib articulated a distinctly different style of music, influenced by the modern khayal format of music and its popular off-shoots, thumri and dadra.

Going back to Bhai Balbir Singh, he was every inch a brilliant Sikh religious musician. He was born on 23rd March 1933, in a family of traditional kirtanias of Tarn Taran area of Amritsar district. As was customary then, he was born in the home of his maternal grandparents in a small village called Mrigindpura near Bhikhiwind in the then Kasur tehsil of Lahore district. This area consisted of the police station of Patti and some more villages that were detached from the Kasur tehsil of Lahore district at the time of independence in 1947 (and later merged with Amritsar district of Indian Punjab). His stout gursikh parents were based in Tarn Taran. He was brought up in the cradle of unadulterated gurmat sangeet of this area.

As explained above, Bhai Balbir Singh, according to his own admission, represented the seventh generation of the Guru-blessed Sikh religious musicians. However, if we go by the criterion of early marriageable age and the average age of reproduction, he could have very well belonged to the thirteenth or fourteenth generation since the time of the fifth Guru.

Some of Bhai Balbir Singh's musician ancestors included his grandfather, Bhai Kundan Singh, a leading musician of the area. His great grandfather was Bhai Inder Singh and his great great grandfather was Bhai Hira Singh. All were well known and highly acclaimed musicians of the Tarn Taran-Amritsar belt. As a child, in addition to the education of music within the family, he was most probably also trained in the gurmat sangeet vidyalaya of Tarn Taran under, among others, by a brilliant teacher of music, Bhai Puran Singh, known for his high-pitched singing. The Tarn Taran area of those days, in fact, was a nursery of music. There were several rababi musician families in the areas surrounding Tarn Taran. Khadoor Sahib had a complete clan of rababis who now live in the city of Lahore. There were other groups in Goindwal Sahib, Sultanpur Lodhi, and Kapurthala too. All these areas contributed musicians to Gurdwara Sri Darbar Sahib in Tarn Taran and Sri Darbar Sahib in Amritsar. Some musicians served in the provincial capital of Lahore in Gurdwara Dera Sahib.

He had inherited a highly melodious, very flexible voice from his father, Bhai Santa Singh, the expert tabla master and kirtania. His father could play several other string instruments as well like the dholaki, mardang, and pakhawaj with equal ease. Taal was, indeed, within the family!

The main profession of this family was doing path and performing shabad kirtan. The philosophy of the family was pure and simple spiritualism, which in their thought process was soaring much higher than the materialistic worldly possessions.

The name of his mother was Bibi Prasinn Kaur, who died when he was not even seven years old. After his mother's untimely death, there was no one in the family to prepare the three meals and there were no materialistic resources to feed the kids. Along with his three younger brothers, he used to show up in the Gurdwara Sri Darbar Sahib's langar hall in Tarn Taran to eat the meals. The top volunteer in-charge of langar always used to mistreat the impoverished brothers, sometimes denying them food. One day, the on-duty musician could not reach on time. Bhai Balbir Singh volunteered to do kirtan then. He performed kirtan of two shabads in perfect sur and taal post which the then raagi took over the stage. The same volunteer for langar had heard Bhai Balbir Singh sing. His voice had gladdened him so much that from that day onwards he never refused langar to him and his siblings.

His elder uncle, Bhai Sohan Singh, was also a known musician at the Golden Temple. Bhai Balbir Singh learnt kirtan from him too. He was so good that at the age of four itself he could take full the alaap and, by the age of seven, he could complete the shabad. He learnt dhrupad from Pandit Nathu Ram, a trainee under Bhai Boota Singh and Baba Shradha Singh.

Bhai Balbir Singh was the eldest and the most accomplished among the four brothers. His formal schooling was up to the eighth grade, but his real education was in music and in remembering more than half of the Sri Guru Granth Sahib and the baani of Sri

Guru Gobind Singh ji as well as the poetry of Bhai Nand Lal Goya and the vars of Bhai Gurdas ji. He could sing the tunes of the great master, Bhai Arjan Singh Tarangar as well as all the 31 raagas mentioned in the Guru Granth Sahib. He had also mastered 250 other raagas and raaginis. He could render each shabad in the prescribed raaga!

He started as a kirtania around 1950 at Sri Darbar Sahib in Tarn Taran. In pursuit of excellence in music, from time to time he visited India's leading gharanas of classical music. Bhai Balbir Singh had a vast knowledge of several reets of the rababi musicians too. His father took great pains to train all his younger brothers in gurmat sangeet to match the talent of their elder brother. Bhai Balbir Singh, too, helped his father in polishing their gurmat sangeet skills.

Prior to the arrival of Bhai Balbir Singh in the holy Sri Darbar Sahib of Amritsar, there was a highly impressive line-up of other iconic kirtanias too. Before 1947, three musicians dominated the scene. They included Bhai Lal rababi, Bhai Chand rababi, and Bhai Santa Singh. Bhai Lal was an accomplished trainer. Bhai Samund Singh, the leading musician of Gurdwara Janam Asthan Sri Nankana Sahib also arrived at the shrine in 1947. However, Bhai Santa Singh left the service in 1949. Soon afterwards Bhai Samund Singh also left the service of Sri Darbar Sahib Amritsar and shifted his residence as a freelancer to Ludhiana.

Sometimes remote inaccessible areas preserve arts and talent remarkably well when the other fast-changing metros lose their purity to the forces of modernisation. Tarn Taran, like Sultanpur Lodhi, was a remote hinterland, quite untouched by the innovations in classical music that had begun to invade the fast-developing cities of Lahore and Amritsar. When Lahore and Amritsar came under the overwhelming spell of khayal gayaki and its lighter offshoots like thumri, dadra, tappa, hori, kajri and kafi during the past two centuries, Tarn Taran and its deep interior were still dominated by the dhrupad and dhamar styles of ancient North Indian classical music. As said earlier, this style dates to the era of the Gurus and before. Partal was a part of ancient classical singing. Bhai Balbir Singh's gayaki reflected the characters of all that he had imbibed in his younger years from within the family and from the other experts of music in his area.

Cramming up a lot of shabads of gurbani was a prerequisite for every Sikh religious musician. This went on side by side with the learning of gurmat sangeet. By the age of twenty, Bhai Balbir Singh had become a complete gurmat musician having mastery over instruments like the tabla, harmonium, jal tarang, dilruba, sitar, violin and other string instruments. His teacher for the jal tarang was a *darvesh*[60] man, Bhai Gian Singh Almast. Bhai Balbir Singh's training was multifaceted as it also included modern khayal gayaki. Tarana, which developed alongside the khayal gayaki, was not only known to him, but he had become a leading exponent of Sri Guru Gobind Singh's own creation of tarana. His command over singing of the tarana won him admiration at many stages but also got him into trouble more than once. Bhai Balbir Singh,

---

[60] Saintly person.

though, was unperturbed. Throughout his long and illustrious career, he never compromised with the classical music that he had studied in his childhood.

Bhai Balbir Singh listened extensively to Bade Ghulam Ali Khan, Nazaqat Ali Khan, and Salamet Ali Khan. He considered both as his mentors. Even Dilip Chandra Vedi was his idol for dhrupad gayaki.

After his two younger brothers were fine-tuned to accompany him, he took his brother, Bhai Chattar Singh, as his second vocal accompaniment on the harmonium, and Bhai Mohinder Singh became his third accompaniment on the tabla.

In 1955, he obtained the most sought-after professional appointment as a hazoori raagi at the Sri Darbar Sahib in Amritsar. The Shiromani Akali Dal and the Shiromani Gurdwara Prabandhak Committee that controlled the historic Sikh shrines were firmly under the stellar leadership of an honest, knowledgeable and popular politician, Master Tara Singh. During those days religious experts like Bhai Vir Singh, Principal Satbir Singh, Bhai Aridaman Singh Bagrian, and Dr Bhai Jodh Singh, the Principal of Khalsa College, Amritsar, used to be consulted for key appointments within the SGPC. The experts of music like Dalip Chander Vedi, Bhai Samund Singh and Bhai Santa Singh were also consulted for the appointment of the key raagis. I am sure the opinion of the Sikh elite must have been sought for Bhai Balbir Singh's appointment as a hazoori raagi.

During those days only a little more than a dozen hazoori musicians were serving the Golden Temple. Bhai Balbir Singh's appointment was hailed by the experts of music and went down in history as one of the last most high-level appointments by the SGPC. After that, roughly from 1962, even the appointments of religious musicians, the pathis, and granthis began to get influenced by politics and was driven by recommendations of those with political power. As time passed, appointments based on merit became lesser and lesser. It is a sad but true commentary on the continuous deterioration of the standard of Sikh clergy in the Golden Temple in Amritsar.

In hindsight, I think that I have heard Bhai Balbir Singh's powerful voice several times over the airwaves of All India Radio Jalandhar during the special early morning services on the Guru Nanak Parkash Gurpurb and Guru Gobind Singh's Parkash Gurpurb after 1956, although the radio station does not formally announce the name of the musician.

Bhai Balbir Singh proved to be an appropriate choice. He was the best exponent of 'Asa Di Vaar'. He could do full justice to every chowki in the shrine. Bhai Balbir Singh trained several budding musicians of the Golden Temple who approached him. They included several senior musicians. Bhai Balbir Singh taught everything with a smile and without a financial motive. He served in the Golden Temple for at least 36 continuous years from 1955 to 1991 with the same members. One of his brothers, Bhai Chattar Singh expired in 1991, but the truncated jatha continued for another four years. This means a continuous service of 40 years at the Golden Temple. He himself continued for another 20 years. This means he served for a total of

60 years[61] albeit with different trainee assistants up to 2015. He was an active kirtania up to the ripe age of 82. After 2015, he drastically curtailed his kirtan duties but was always ready to teach.

While serving in Sri Darbar Sahib in Amritsar, Bhai Balbir Singh used to be sent to other places on special assignments. His lineage comprised of brave Sikhs who, even when outnumbered, fought valiantly and often defeated the enemy.

As told to me by a historian of Sikh religious music, Dr Kanwaljit Singh, on one such special assignment, Bhai Balbir Singh was performing shabad kirtan at Gurdwara Sri Sis Ganj Sahib in Old Delhi. It was the 1st November 1984. After the assassination of Mrs Indira Gandhi, Delhi was very tense. A huge mob of rioters made a bid to invade the historic gurdwara. Bhai Balbir Singh and his jatha stopped the kirtan abruptly and walked downstairs brandishing naked three-foot-long swords kept in the historic gurdwara. On seeing the advancing high spirited jatha, the rioters panicked and dispersed in the by-lanes. After that Bhai Sahib started to perform the kirtan all over again in perfect *charhdi kala*.[62] The crowd of scared Sikhs showered a lot

---

[61] The other long-term musicians included Bhai Samund Singh of Gurdwara Janam Asthan Sri Nankana Sahib from 1912 to 1947 for 35 years. Bhai Santa Singh served the Golden Temple from 1925 to 1949, nearly for 25 years, and Bhai Avtar Singh Gurcharan Singh served Gurdwara Sri Sis Ganj Sahib in Old Delhi from 1952 to 1990 for nearly 38 years. Bhai Avtar Singh served after that too till his death, but without Bhai Gurcharan Singh, who had become too old and had difficulty in sitting for long hours. Now Bhai Avtar Singh's son, Bhai Kultar Singh, assisted by his cousin, Bhai Swaran Singh, does the kirtan sewa at Delhi's historic gurdwaras.

[62] *Charhdi kala*: The attempt to maintain a mental state of eternal optimism and joy

of money on the courageous raagi jatha.

While serving at the Golden Temple, he travelled to most of the other leading centres of music in India. The places which he visited and where he learnt from the others included Lucknow, Benares, Gwalior, Agra, Poona, Calcutta, Meerut and Delhi. He exchanged his sea of knowledge with the experts of the host gharanas. He learnt the finer points of singing from Pandit Krishan Rao of Gwalior and obtained valuable tips on classical music from Padma Shri Janab Habib Ud Din Khan of Meerut. In return, Bhai Balbir Singh taught them the difference between Shastriya sangeet and the gurmat sangeet. Bhai Balbir Singh and Ustad Gian Singh Almast were very good friends. Bhai Balbir Singh's father was a good teacher of dilruba, saranda, veena and taus, but Gian Singh Almast was a magician of the jal tarang, which he taught to Bhai Balbir Singh.

Satguru Jagjit Singh of the Naamdhari Sampardaya was a great admirer of gurmat sangeet. He held Bhai Balbir Singh in very high esteem. Many times, he invited Bhai Balbir Singh to his place in Bhaini Sahib and heard him with utter humility for hours. He even instructed his own raagi jathas to learn the finer points of gurmat sangeet from him.

Bhai Balbir Singh's biggest misfortune was that most of his professional years were spent in and around Tarn Taran and Amritsar. The Nihang Singh type dress code of his brothers forming the raagi jatha also did not meet the standard of acceptance by the urban sangat.

His contemporary, Bhai Bakhshish Singh, was a much more widely-travelled man and that gave him worldwide exposure. Once while living in the USA, I tried to sponsor Bhai Balbir Singh's raagi jatha to visit the United States through a third party, but he very politely declined the invitation. He did the same to an invitation from the Canadian Sikhs too. He was happy in his own comfort zone. Personally, he was a real artist and a highly contented man, and such a man cannot amass wealth like the present-day business-oriented half-trained make-shift musicians can. Bhai Balbir Singh's more recent proteges include Bhai Sarbjit Singh Laadi, a former hazoori raagi of Sri Darbar Sahib Amritsar, and his own son, Bhai Bahadur Singh. Both of them are in great demand abroad. Financially they are doing better than Bhai Balbir Singh. One of his most well-trained musicians is Bhai Nirmal Singh of Batala. He sings quite like Bhai Balbir Singh.

Though he was born in Lahore district, up to 1947, he had not seen Lahore, and after that Lahore became an alien territory. Looking at his strong musical credentials, Bhai Balbir Singh was not financially as sound as he should and could have been. He owned a modest house in the Antarjami Colony on Tarn Taran Road of Amritsar. His music was his hobby and obsession. He could spend hours in the company of musicians. The lovers of music in Delhi were his strength.

I know about only three musicians who refused to alter their style of music in the face of the ever-changing musical scene around them. Bhai Balbir Singh was the foremost among them. The other two included the Late Bhai Santa Singh, who stood his ground firmly when his old assistant musician, Bhai Surjan Singh, switched to the simple, non-traditional style of music to please the unsophisticated rural and urban folks. At one time it appeared that Bhai Santa Singh's style would become extinct after his death in 1966, but as the people living in Delhi became financially well off, their tastes of fine arts, including music, also became richer. After his death, his brothers, Bhai Shamsher Singh and Bhai Jabarjang Singh, carried forward his traditions for a few years and then his nephews, Bhai Harjit Singh and Gurdeep Singh, did the same and this has continued into the present day as well. Bhai Mangal Singh also learnt gurmat sangeet from Bhai Santa Singh. Now his brilliant son, Bhai Manohar Singh, keeps Bhai Santa Singh's style alive, albeit with slight modifications.

Bhai Jwala Singh's style of ancient gurmat sangeet was kept alive by his sons, Bhai Avtar Singh and Bhai Gurcharan Singh. They bluntly refused to change. After their deaths, now Bhai Jwala Singh's, grandson, Bhai Kultar Singh, along with his cousin, Bhai Swaran Singh, are keeping their ancient traditions alive. So far, they are popular among the knowledgeable and wealthy Sikh elite of Delhi. Even in the USA, Canada, the UK and Malaysia, their style finds acceptance. Another member of their extended family, Bhai Baldeep Singh, has become a well-meaning historian of Sikh religious music. He is good at making old instruments like the saranda, taus and the rabab, all of which have been used in Sikh religious music. It was only with Bhai Baldeep Singh's efforts, that he received the highest Government of India award from the Sangeet Natak Academy.

Bhai Balbir Singh taught some part of his vast treasure of gurmat sangeet to his sons, Bhai Bahadur

Singh and Bhai Saudagar Singh. Despite this, I have my doubts whether they will be able to match their father's knowledge of the centuries-old gurmat sangeet. I have more hope from his grandsons, Bhai Harsimran Singh and Bhai Sat Simran Singh. They are much better educated, and if encouraged properly, can do a lot.

The art of tarana singing, evolved by the tenth master, Guru Gobind Singh ji, is now alive with another brilliant musician, Bhai Gurmeet Singh Shant, a former hazoori raagi of the Golden Temple. Even Bhai Bakhshish Singh had some reets of gurmat sangeet common with Bhai Balbir Singh.

Once Bhai Gurcharan Singh, son of Bhai Jwala Singh, in a casual remark exclaimed that Bhai Balbir Singh is like a deep well, the more water one draws out the more remains behind. It is impossible to estimate the quantum of his reservoir of music. Sardar Jodh Singh, a brilliant, retired assistant station director of All India Radio Jalandhar, once admitted that the radio station could not fully explore his vast potential as an instrumentalist and as a vocalist. He felt that the station could have done a lot more, like recording his rendition of the jal tarang, dilruba, taus, saranda, veena, violin and also the solo performances on the tabla. Rajinder Pal Singh Rana, a one-time music composer at All India Radio Jalandhar once remarked that Bhai Balbir Singh is an unmatched ustad kirtania and that he was a breed apart from all his contemporaries.

Bhai Balbir Singh was a very humorous character. He joked about himself too. However, every great man has a drawback. He was very shy of unknown environments and mixing with strangers. This disability came in the way of his long-term professional ascendancy. He was, at times, moody too. He was an artist who had been approved long ago by All India Radio Jalandhar. When it had lost its original paperwork regarding the audition of Bhai Balbir Singh, they invited him to visit the radio station once again to renew his credentials. However, on the appointed day and time, Bhai Balbir Singh simply refused to show up, saying that he had already been approved, and it was outrightly insulting to appear all over again. This led to a lot of disappointment in the radio station staff, who wanted to help him. I enquired from All India Radio Jalandhar about the recordings of Bhai Balbir Singh in their library. They have eight of his rare renditions.

He never hankered after money and materialistic pleasures. He visited only two countries outside India. One was Thailand and the second was Malaysia, including Kuala Lumpur and Singapore. The gurdwaras in the United Kingdom, especially in Birmingham and Southall, were longing for his visit, but Bhai Balbir Singh was totally disinterested in undertaking foreign tours. The same is true of his reluctance in touring Vancouver and Toronto in Canada.

Punjab slipped into an indecisive phase when, in June 1984, the notorious Operation Blue Star occurred in the Golden Temple, resulting in unprecedented bloodshed and the destruction of the centuries old heritage complex. Soon thereafter, the then Prime Minister, Indira Gandhi, went into overdrive to please the angry Sikh psyche. In a jiffy, she ordered the daily broadcast of live kirtan from the sanctum sanctorum of Sri Darbar Sahib by All India Radio Jalandhar. The first slot was of 'Asa Di Vaar' from 4 a.m. to 6 a.m. on medium-wave 343.6 meters corresponding to 873 kilohertz. This was the pre-dawn time when the medium-wave signal from the radio station could reach every part of India and most parts of the Middle Eastern countries as well. Bhai Balbir Singh got more than his fair share of early morning kirtan slots for broadcasts from the station.

The other was a one-hour long slot from 4:30 p.m. to 5:30 p.m. in the afternoon on the same frequency but during the daylight hours. Its primary range was about one hundred kilometres. My late mother, Mrs Harjit Kaur, thoroughly enjoyed the morning slot, whenever Bhai Balbir Singh was on duty. A lot of Sindhi followers of Guru Nanak in India and Pakistan enjoyed hearing the gurmat sangeet rendered by Bhai Balbir Singh. For years things were fine. One fact was conspicuous that in the years after the 1960s, the taste for gurmat sangeet in Punjab had been sliding down. Even the management of the SGPC developed a lackadaisical attitude towards the preservation of a decent standard.

His raagi jatha at Sri Darbar Sahib in Amritsar consisted originally of his immediate family members. One of his brothers, Bhai Chattar Singh, was the second singer with the harmonium as the instrument. His other brother, Bhai Mohinder Singh used to accompany him on the tabla – the combination was perfect. All the lovers of good music in and around Amritsar started enjoying his performances. During the 1950s and 60s, he was held in high esteem. When one of his brothers died in 1991, and then after the second one died too, his dependence on others increased. Between 1995 and

2015, he was accompanied by his short term shagirds.

He was the most important participant, year after year, at the annual classical kirtan darbar on the birth anniversary of the fourth master, Sri Guru Ram Das ji, at Gurdwara Manji Sahib Diwan Hall in Amritsar. On some occasions, Bhai Didar of Nangal Khurd district Hoshiarpur attended this very kirtan darbar. He was all praise for the overall brilliance of Bhai Balbir Singh.

Bhai Balbir Singh got several awards and honours in his life. In 1987, the Kendri Singh Sabha in Chandigarh honoured him in a special gathering. The Jawaddi Taksal, dedicated to classical music, conferred the Shiromani Kirtania award on Bhai Balbir Singh in 1991. In 1993, the Indian Council of Sikh Affairs honoured him. Sant Sujan Singh Kirtan Society conferred its lifetime achievement award on him in 1994. Bhai Mardana Kirtan Society gave him its award in 1995. The then President of India, Mr Narayanan gave him an award in 1996. The Bhai Batan Singh Memorial Award was conferred on him in 1997. He was also named the Shiromani Kirtania in some other functions. The Gurmat Sangeet Award was given to him by Jawaddi Taksal in 1999. The language department of Punjab conferred the title of Shiromani Kirtania on him in 2001. Sant Sarwan Singh Gandharav Award was conferred on him in 2001. The Shiromani Gurdwara Prabandhak Committee Amritsar also conferred the title of Shiromani Kirtania on him in 2004. The Bhai Mardana Gurmat Sangeet Society of British Midlands honoured him in 2006. Bhai Dilbagh Singh Kirtania Award was bestowed on him by the Guru Nanak Dev University Amritsar in 2010. There are many other organisations that have conferred honours on him.

By far the biggest admirer of Bhai Balbir Singh was Sant Sucha of village Jawaddi in Ludhiana. As long as he was alive, he invited Bhai Balbir Singh every year and gave him a lot of respect. He knew how to get the best out of Bhai Balbir Singh. Under his patronage, Bhai Balbir Singh sang 'Asa Di Vaar' in a three-cassette set. This is a landmark rendition of 'Asa Di Vaar'.

The owner family of the T-Series recording company of Delhi was a big admirer of the talent of Bhai Balbir Singh. They were refugees from Pakistan, who settled in New Delhi in 1947. As a financial compensation for recording his music, they always paid him more than double the money compared to the other musicians. They did a lot of his recordings. They had asked him that whenever he would be in Delhi, he should get some recordings done. Some of these recordings are on YouTube now.

Sant Sucha Singh's successor, Bhai Ameer Singh, also invited Bhai Balbir Singh every year to the annual function in the *taksal*.[63] Some of his most relaxed recordings were made in the Jawaddi Taksal. The Namdhari Guru, Jagjit Singh, too was a great admirer of Bhai Balbir Singh's gurmat sangeet. He always asked his kirtanias to follow Bhai Balbir Singh's style of kirtan.

Bhai Balbir Singh believed that to err is human and to forgive is God. According to the Sikh way of life, if someone commits a mistake, he should appear before Sri Akal Takhat, make an admission of his/her guilt, accept the punishment awarded by Sri Akal Takhat,

[63] seminary

undergo that punishment, and then lead a normal guilt-free life. Most devout Sikhs follow this way of life.

The winter of 2020 was a severe and prolonged one in Punjab and the other northern states of India. On 23 February, just one month short of Bhai Balbir Singh's birthday (he would have turned 87 years old on 23 March), due to some age- and weather-related complications, he died a natural death in his modest cottage on Tarn Taran Road in Amritsar. Most of his admirers outside Amritsar did not know about his demise. As is a common practice in India, the iconic musician was cremated on the same day. It can be said that he was born as a *faqir* – a carefree, God-fearing, poor soul – and was cremated like one. His *bhog*[64] took place on 2 March 2020. By the time of his bhog, his son, Bhai Bahadar Singh, and his favourite protégé, Bhai Sarbjit Singh Laadi, who were abroad, came back. The SGPC in Amritsar, for whom he had served for six long decades, was present in full force. The venue of his bhog was full to its capacity (it can accommodate 2,000 people). The memorial function was conducted by Bhai Sarbjit Singh Laadi. The main musician in attendance was Bhai Nirmal Singh Khalsa, who also coincidently died exactly a month later on 2 April 2020, from complications that arose due to the Coronavirus infection. Some other leading musicians, who paid their respects to the departed soul, included hazoori raagis of Sri Darbar Sahib, Bhai Nirmal Singh of Batala, Bhai

---

[64] In Sikhism, it is used for observances that are fulfilled along with the reading of the concluding part of the Sri Guru Granth Sahib. It can be performed in conjunction with weddings, obsequies, anniversaries, funeral services and other occasions when a family or a worshipping community may consider such a reading appropriate. (Wikipedia)

Kamaljit Singh, Bhai Gurmel Singh, Bhai Gurmej Singh, and Bhai Ravinder Singh. Bhai Balbir Singh's grandsons, Bhai Harsimran Singh and Bhai Sat Simran Singh also performed kirtan. Due to limitations of time, most other musicians did not get a chance to sing.

Bhai Balbir Singh dedicated his entire life to gurmat sangeet. He served Gurdwara Sri Darbar Sahib in Tarn Taran for at least five years from 1950 to 1955. He served Gurdwara Sri Darbar Sahib in Amritsar uninterrupted from 1955 to 1991 with an unchanged raagi jatha and up to 1995 with a change in the composition of his group. From 1995 to 2015, for a span of another 20 years, he served Sri Darbar Sahib Amritsar when his services were needed. All his service was under the SGPC and DSGMC. He trained scores of musicians and was training someone till his last breath as well. Such a person deserves to be honoured and celebrated. His portrait deserves to be installed in the Central Sikh Museum. A museum of music should also be built in his memory in Amritsar. He was the last of the old guard of puritan gurmat sangeet.

Jathedar Gurcharan Singh Tohra

Around the early 1960s, there was a change in the leadership of the Shiromani Akali Dal. A long-time incumbent, Master Tara Singh, was ousted from the Presidency of Shiromani Akali Dal and was replaced by Sant Fateh Singh. His close lieutenant, Sant Channan Singh, was elected the President of the SGPC. Both had much lower educational credentials compared to their better-experienced predecessor. This was just the beginning of the downslide in the standard of music in the Golden Temple too.

During the 1970s, a no-nonsense administrator, Jathedar Gurcharan Singh Tohra, became the President of the SGPC. He cared little about the seniority of the musicians and took severe disciplinary actions when the slightest of mistakes were committed.

One morning, one of Tohra sahib's well-wishers was listening to the 'Asa Di Vaar' on his radio. Bhai Balbir Singh was performing the shabad kirtan. After a few chhakkas, he used to sing a complete classical *bandish*.[65] He had crammed up a lot of gurbani of Sri Guru Gobind Singh ji too (which is not included in the Sri Guru Granth Sahib ji). He usually rendered the writings of Bhai Nand Lal Goya in praise of Sri Guru Gobind Singh ji. While rendering a shabad, he started reciting a tarana composed by the Master himself. The grammar and meters of that particular tarana resembled some dancing steps too. Obviously, that person had no sense of classical music, and in a fit of rage, he shot off an angry letter to Tohra sahib complaining about the musician on duty. The guy precisely wrote that the musician was luring the listeners to dance. After reading this letter, Tohra sahib was angry and enquired from the staff of the SGPC about the name of the musician on 'Asa Di Vaar' duty in Sri Darbar Sahib. Bhai Balbir Singh's name popped up. Without caring for the highly admirable credentials and impeccable seniority of Bhai Balbir Singh, he was placed under suspension!

After this incident, Jathedar Gurcharan Singh Tohra came on a visit to the United States. When I met

[65] A fixed, melodic composition in Hindustani vocal or instrumental music.

him personally, I raised the issue of the suspension of Bhai Balbir Singh. He told me about the letter that he had received. I had two questions for him. My first question was, 'How knowledgeable was the letter writer about classical music or gurmat sangeet?' and my second question was 'Have you heard Sri Guru Gobind Singh ji's tarana?'. His answer to both questions was in the negative. That is when I told him about the credentials of Bhai Balbir Singh who had been appointed a hazoori raagi more than fifteen years before Jathedar Gurcharan Singh Tohra's election as the President of SGPC and he was by far the senior-most musician. This revelation opened Jathedar Tohra's eyes. For a moment he pondered over his action. Soon after Bhai Balbir Singh was reinstated. Those who loved gurmat sangeet and were admirers of Bhai Balbir Singh approved the new decision taken by Jathedar Gurcharan Singh Tohra. Of course, politics is dirty everywhere, even in places of worship. There were unprofessional musicians too in the service of the SGPC, who were unhappy at Bhai Balbir Singh's reinstatement but he was above such petty interferences.

During the early 1980s, Jathedar Gurcharan Singh Tohra lost the de-facto control of the SGPC, though, on paper, he remained the President.

10

Bhai Dharam Singh Zakhmi

A Great Preacher of Kirtania

Since the days of Sri Guru Nanak Dev ji and his lifelong musician assistant, Bhai Mardana (a Muslim rababi maestro), there has been a long association of the rababi Muslim musicians with the Sikh community. Around 1,000 years ago, the rababi families consisted primarily of hereditary musicians and one of them, Bhai Mardana, enjoyed the unique privilege of becoming a lifelong musical assistant of Sri Guru Nanak Dev ji. He accompanied the great Guru during his four famous journeys. Long after the death of the last Sikh Guru, Sri Guru Gobind Singh, in 1708, this community of professional musicians kept the traditions of original shabad kirtan tunes and formats alive by performing gurmat sangeet in the gurdwaras and homes of the followers of the faith. Most of the rababi musicians kept on performing shabad kirtan till the beginning of the twentieth century in the original tunes of the Guru darbars. Even while serving the Sikh audiences, most maintained their strong association with their Islamic faith, but some of them became genuinely attracted towards the Sikh faith and they eventually became practising Sikhs.

Most of the more accomplished rababi musician families lived in the districts of Amritsar, Lahore, Nankana Sahib, Jullundur, Hoshiarpur and Kapurthala. During the twentieth century, some of the rababi kirtanias living in Amritsar, Jullundur, Hoshiarpur and Nankana Sahib had converted to the Sikh faith. Bhai Dharam Singh Zakhmi's name was one of the most prominent among them. He became an amritdhari Sikh in 1947 by properly grasping the basics of the religion and after getting fully committed to his new faith. Since then, his family and he never looked back. Over the years, and after reading the best Farsi and Urdu books on the religion, Bhai Dharam Singh Zakhmi had acquired a deep understanding of preaching the Sikh faith. While in school, he had studied Urdu and Persian languages and learnt history and philosophy as subjects through the old Persian and Urdu books on the subject. His pronunciation of Urdu words was perfect. This was greatly appreciated by the educated and knowledgeable audiences in the Sikh congregations. After Bhai Samund Singh, Bhai Dharam Singh Zakhmi came to be recognised as the other most respected Sikh religious musician of All India Radio Jalandhar. Being a scholar of the Sikh religion and a leading orator, Bhai Dharam Singh Zakhmi became a very popular kathakar too and as such he earned a lot of name and fame.

Bhai Dharam Singh Zakhmi was born and brought up in a nondescript village Manko (near Adampur) in Jalandhar district. His younger brother, Bhai Shamsher Singh Zakhmi, had worked even harder on classical music and his voice became very sweet and flexible. His range of produced notes was also very extensive. He could easily modulate between the highest and the lowest notes. As such during the later years of the group, Bhai Shamsher Singh Zakhmi used to virtually lead the party in singing. In earlier years both brothers used to complement each other. When most of the other raagi jathas performed shabad kirtan as groups of three – two on harmoniums and one on tabla – Bhai Dharam Singh Zakhmi's group had a string instrument too and it consisted of four musicians.

Bhai Dharam Singh Zakhmi's initial training in classical music took place within the family. Later on, for intensive training, he became the student of Professor Darshan Singh Komal of Hoshiarpur. The blind maestro trained scores of Sikh religious musicians. Among his most promising shagirds were Bhai Dharam singh Zakhmi, Bhai Didar Singh (another great blind maestro), Bhai Beant Singh Bijli, and Bhai Gian Singh Surjeet (also a blind artist). One of Bhai Dharam Singh Zakhmi's sons, Bhai Amrik Singh Zakhmi was trained to play the string instrument, dilruba, and another brother of Bhai Dharam Singh, Har Iqbal Singh, accompanied the group as a tabla player. Even the legendry Bhai Samund Singh ji loved to hear some of the shabads in the choicest reets rendered by Bhai Dharam Singh Zakhmi's group. Bhai Dharam Singh Zakhmi's party was one of the first among the Sikh musicians to travel abroad. Among other countries, they visited Kenya, the United Kingdom, Malaysia and Singapore several times. During one of their trips to Great Britain, the audiences liked their kirtan so much that they had to extend their two-month trip to more than six months! Some of their music was recorded on professional spool-type tape decks. However, regularly transcription of their renditions was done during their tours of Singapore.

Bhai Dharam Singh Zakhmi died around 1978 and after a few months, his group was taken over by his younger brother, Bhai Shamsher Singh Zakhmi. Gurdwara Richmond Hill sponsored the visit of the raagi jatha of Bhai Shamsher Singh Zakhmi in 1985. After serving in that famous gurdwara for six weeks, the group visited Gurdwara

Bridgewater New Jersey for a month. During this trip, the second singer was another rababi maestro, Bhai Mohan Pal Singh, formerly of Gurdwara Janam Asthan Sri Nankana Sahib and the drummer was Akal Singh, a nephew of Bhai Dharam Singh Zakhmi. During that trip, Bhai Mohan Pal Singh's performance was simply outstanding. A lot of Bhai Dharam Singh Zakhmi's music has been very well recorded and a substantial part is now available on the internet under Gurmarsangeetproject.com and Keertan.org. Bhai Dharam Singh Zakhmi is not with us anymore, but his voice lives on for the benefit of the future generations of listeners of good music.

Bhai Dharam Singh Zakhmi is third from left

11

Bhai Didar Singh

A Selfless and Highly Accomplished Sikh Musician Who Deserves More Appreciation

Bhai Didar Singh was a totally selfless faqir kirtania, who devoted his entire life to the singing of the Guru's hymns in the finest classical traditions without seeking any monetary rewards. He lived in poverty and died in poverty, without ever complaining about his plight. Most of the modern-day Sikhs have forgotten him completely, but his merit as a maestro and his extreme simplicity must be told.

During the 1960s my father, Late S. Sochet Singh, once attended a post akhand paath kirtan programme in rural Hoshiarpur. He was a true connoisseur of gurmat sangeet and was thoroughly impressed with the sweet, versatile voice of a blind, black-bearded, young musician named Bhai Didar Singh. After that cursory reference, I did not hear about this maestro. He was never heard of in a kirtan darbar, or at any private religious function. To me his name was a faint memory that remained dormant in a remote corner of my brain for years to come.

Around 1983 someone in Vancouver gave me a tape with the handwritten title 'Bhai Didar Singh raagi' on its cover. On hearing an enchanting unheard-of voice, the old memories of my father's words sprouted up again. The longest duration shabad in the tape was titled 'Aappe bauh bidh rangla, sakhiye mera laal'. It turned out to be a very professionally rendered shabad in a difficult-to-perform *Guldasta* format and it simply mesmerised me. I listened to this tape again and again and still did not get tired of it. I made a spare copy of this tape to guard against any damage to the original tape.

Bhai Didar Singh lived most of his life in the village Nangal Khurd in Hoshiarpur District. On the death of his illustrious teacher, Ustad Darshan Singh Komal, Bhai Didar Singh became the successor of his legacy. He continued to teach shabad kirtan to the prospecting raagis. Occasionally, he visited foreign lands too.

A few months later, after I had heard his voice on the tape, I met Giani Gurdip Singh ji, the then head priest of the Gurdwara Richmond Hill in New York. This gurdwara was a de-facto place of pilgrimage for all the Sikhs living North of Washington D.C. on the eastern seaboard of America. I made a casual mention of this newly-obtained tape to him and his eyes lit up. He was very knowledgeable, and he had already heard this tape. He told me that Darshan Singh Komal had had three highly accomplished shagirds. One out of them had been Bhai Dharam Singh Zakhmi who was very comfortable in lower musical notes. Among the others, Bhai Beant Singh Bijli was more comfortable in higher notes, but Bhai Didar Singh was so versatile that he could move with great ease between the highest and the lowest notes and always did full justice to the intricacies of raaga. Bhai Gurdip Singh further said Bhai Didar Singh's voice was something similar to that of K.L. Saigal and Bade Ustad Ghulam Ali Khan!

A few months later, I talked to Rabinder Singh Bhamra, the scholarly Vice President of Gurdwara Richmond Hill in New York. He told me that their gurdwara management had sponsored Bhai Didar Singh's jatha's visit to New York in the second half of 1984. Bhai Didar Singh, at the head of a four-man raagi jatha, had come in October. Sardar Tejinder Singh Kahlon, the long-time president of that gurdwara told me that Bhai Didar Singh had stayed at the Gurdwara Richmond Hill for one-and-a-half months and after that, I was allowed to take his raagi jatha to Gurdwara Bridgewater, New Jersey. I was thrilled to hear about the offer and on the appointed day I drove this jatha to Gurdwara Bridgewater. This was in December.

Gurdwara Richmond Hill is approximately 80 miles away from Gurdwara Bridgewater and it was a good two hours plus journey. I had several questions to ask, and Bhai Didar Singh had the answers. I seated him on the front seat and his three companions – Ajit Singh, Sarbjit Singh, and Sukhdev Singh – were seated at the back. I started the curious conversation by asking about his initiation into classical music or gurmat sangeet. He told me that he being blind had a lot of handicaps. A blind man cannot read or write, so he was made to cram up as much gurbani as possible before attaining the age of ten. Hence, by the age of 12, he had crammed up more than 800 shabads. These shabads, he told me, he still remembered and sang. He went on to add that roughly at the age of ten, he was initiated into classical music and by the age of 15, he had become adept in the rendition of close to 80 raagas and raaginis. Bhai Didar Singh told me that learning a raaga is the easy part. It was its repeated riyaz and sticking to its true character like the discrete application of komal and teevar surs which was the most difficult part of its rendition. He said that he had done riyaz for several hours every day till the age of 25 but after that, the hours had gotten reduced and, instead the daily kirtan in different raagas had taken over. Despite this, he said, he always managed to do some riyaz. Bhai Didar Singh also told me that he could proficiently play most of the taals on the tabla.

In addition, he was also groomed to play two string instruments – the sarangi and the violin. His ustad, Professor Darshan Singh Komal, trained him as a versatile musician and taught him to play the sarangi with ease. According to his tutor, the sarangi was an instrument that would come to his rescue during the worst of times. After imparting adequate knowledge in singing and instrument playing, his ustad established him as the lead singer and he became his *saathi* on the tabla.

At one extremely bad time in his life, the sarangi indeed came to his rescue. When no one wanted to listen to classical music, he improvised a *dhadi* jatha[66] wherein he became the sarangi player and two of his students became the dhadi singers. This hurriedly assembled rag-tag dhadi jatha became very popular in rural Punjab within a very short duration, and this switch over earned him a lot more money than he

[66] A band of dhadis or ballad singers who use the dhadd and the sarangi during singing.

had been earning as a professionally-trained kirtania.

He told me that he had brought a sarangi for that tour also and confided in me that he had done so because he felt that there were probably places in America where proper classical kirtan may not find acceptance. He said that at such places the sarangi would come to his rescue, and that his new companions who had come with him on the tour, Sarbjit Singh and Sukhdev Singh, had been trained as dhadis as well.

Bhai Didar Singh lamented that since the 1960s, the appreciation and respect for real good musicians had been declining steadily. Those with virtually no training and having uncultured voices, but possessing good managerial skills, were in great demand. He felt sad that the genuinely skilled musicians were struggling.

During our journey, I also asked him why his voice had never been heard on the airwaves of All India Radio to which he replied that nobody from the radio station ever approached him and the idea of going uninvited to the radio station never occurred to him. However, he said that some of the folks who took lessons in music from him had already become radio artists. Later, I did hear his voice on All India Radio Jalandhar.

In an answer to another question, Bhai Didar Singh said that he had been invited every year to perform shabad gayan during the famous Guru Ram Dass Birth Anniversary Kirtan Darbar at the Gurdwara Manji Sahib located within the Golden Temple complex, but his shabad kirtan had never been broadcasted from the sanctum sanctorum of the Temple. He said that some genuine lovers of music in Punjab had really given him a lot of respect and he was thankful to them.

Bhai Didar Singh was all praise for Late Bhai Samund Singh ji. According to him, Bhai Samund Singh was the only kirtania who would render all the shabads in a chowki in pure classical formats, whereas everybody else rendered the first shabad in a classical raaga and then switched to the semi-classical or the light reets.

In reply to another question, Bhai Didar Singh said that he had a lot of admiration for rababi kirtanias. He felt that they had certain advantages too. Being musicians by profession, their kids got introduced to the pakka raag at a very young age. This grooming gave them a lifelong advantage.

The two hours just flew by and we reached the parking area of Gurdwara Bridgewater. We were not sure of the sangat's response to his voice and art, but contrary to our fears, the weekly Friday and Sunday congregations at Gurdwara Bridgewater thoroughly appreciated his kirtan kala and he was not compelled to use his sarangi as a dhadi during any of the diwans.

Bhai Pargat Singh, a long-time resident of New York, is a well-trained classical musician. He has learnt proper classical music from a highly accomplished classical maestro, Master Rattan of Phagwara. He is also a great connoisseur of all kinds of classical music. Bhai Didar Singh was one of his most favourite kirtanias. I invited Bhai Pargat Singh to an evening of kirtan darbar at the Gurdwara Bridgewater. He was asked to bring his taanpura too. He came with his musician family. Together, they performed a very melodious kirtan. After that, he accompanied Bhai Didar Singh also, as a side musician, with his taanpura. This performance came out to be a historic event. I am glad I have been able to preserve its transcript.

During his month-long stay at the Gurdwara Bridgewater, Bhai Didar Singh invariably performed the first shabad in pure khayali classical format and the subsequent ones were rendered in reets based on various classical raagas.

I personally made a number of recordings of his renditions.

Before we could schedule his repeat visit in 1989, he had passed away. He was diabetic and no one in India got his heart checked as we do in America. He died before attaining the age of 60. He is not physically with us anymore, but his voice lives on. Bhai Didar Singh was truly a master Sikh religious musician who deserved more appreciation than he got.

12

Bhai Prithipal Singh and Mohan Pal Singh

A Link with the Musical Heritage of Nankana Sahib

Since the days of Maharaja Ranjit Singh's empire, Gurdwara Janam Asthan Sri Nankana Sahib and Sri Darbar Sahib Amritsar have been acknowledged to be the two shrines where the Sikh musical heritage was preserved at its pristine and sophisticated best. Other historic shrines used to look to these great places of worship for inspiration and guidance. Sri Darbar Sahib is with us, and we have extensively heard gurmat sangeet by the musicians in its service. We know this music since the days of Bhai Santa Singh and his contemporaries. We have also heard the music of Bhai Samund Singh ji of Sri Nankana Sahib, but other than him, we have not been really conversant with what his other contemporaries were singing.

This made me curious to know about the others, and, in particular, how the famous rababi kirtanias, used to sing gurbani at the Gurdwara Janam Asthan Sri Nankana Sahib. I got lucky when I stumbled upon a musician, who represented the second generation of the refugee raagis from Nankana Sahib. This happened in 1976 when I was posted as a Sub-Divisional Engineer (Construction) at Patiala. Police buildings in Fort Bahadurgarh were under my charge.

I observed a large Sikh man, wearing white clothes, coming out of Gurdwara Bahadurgarh Sahib. This gurdwara is situated on the opposite side of Fort Bahadurgarh. A man who knew this individual told me that he was the finest classical musician in Patiala, and introduced him as Bhai Mohan Pal Singh.

The extrovert that I am, I tried talking with this mysterious musician. He quickly judged my curiosity and asked me if I had heard about Bhai Pal Singh, Jaswant Singh, Bhai Gurmukh Singh, and Bhai Sarmukh Singh Fakkar of Sri Nankana Sahib? When I answered in the affirmative, he told me that he was one of the descendants of this great family of musicians. However, he wanted me to hear him first and then decide if he could be considered a worthy descendent of the famous kirtanias of the yore. I asked him if he knew the reets, in which Bhai Pal Singh and Jaswant Singh used to sing at Nankana Sahib. He nodded his head and told me that he could. He then gave me his address, but he had no phone.

One fine holiday morning I decided to see him at his residence. He lived in a poor neighbourhood called Tripuri in Patiala city. The street leading to his home was only partly paved, the rest was potholed, muddy, and dusty with milch cattle tied on both sides. On reaching his home I knocked at his door. The unpainted door was opened by Bhai Mohan Pal Singh himself. He was happy to receive me. He asked his lady to warm the milk for the guest, but I refused. He asked a young boy, who looked around 12, to bring the tabla.

That day he sang 'Bilaskhani Todi'. From his alaap, it seemed to me that he was a pupil of Ustad Bade Ghulam Ali Khan, which he later proudly admitted that he was. He told me that during the early 1960s, his cousin, Prithipal Singh, and he were sent to Khan Sahib Bade Ghulam Ali Khan in Bombay to learn the finer points of the singing traditions of the Patiala Gharana and the training helped them a lot professionally. Ever since that training, he and his cousin had been doing riyaz of what they had learnt.

While in Bombay, they met the legendary playback singer, Mohammad Rafi, who offered them lucrative assignments as chorus singers in the film industry, but they politely rejected them saying that they didn't want to quit their ancestral profession of singing for their Guru. They both kept visiting Malerkotla to learn more about music from Ustad Bakar Ali Khan, the most accomplished music teacher of the Patiala Gharana. I was impressed. My father (Late Sardar Sochet Singh) lived in Chandigarh. During his college days at the Lahore Government College, he occasionally visited Nankana Sahib and was impressed with the singing skills of the rababi kirtanias of Gurdwara Janam Asthan. He was, hence, quite curious to hear the voices of their descendants. I promised him that I would bring them to Chandigarh for a special kirtan diwan at my father's residence. I never got the chance to do so as my father passed away on 31 August 1976. He could not hear them sing, but they were present and even performed kirtan on his *antim*[67] ardas.

Bhai Mohan Pal Singh kept telling me that his cousin, Bhai Prithipal Singh, was an even better kirtania than him. While in Patiala, I did not have the privilege of listening to Bhai Prithipal Singh and a desire to listen to him remained in my heart. I often used to go to Gurdwara Sri Dukh Niwaran Sahib at Patiala where I used to hear Bhai Joginder Singh and Mohinder Singh, the cousins of Bhai Mohan Pal Singh and Prithipal Singh, perform gurmat sangeet. They were truly mesmerising. After coming to America, I had the privilege, in 1985, of inviting Bhai Mohan Pal Singh, who was accompanying Bhai Shamsher Singh Zakhmi, to

[67] last

perform shabad kirtan at Gurdwara Bridgewater New Jersey. I made some recordings too. Bhai Mohan Pal Singh's voice was power-packed and highly cultured.

A while ago, a friend of mine guided me to listen to Sikh devotional music on *longislandkirtan.com*. I did and to my surprise in the folder titled 'Old Vintage Kirtan', I stumbled upon some recordings in the voice of Bhai Prithipal Singh. It has the 'Asa Di Vaar' in two parts and there are 2 more MP-3s in the voice of this musician. After listening to these four folders, I found in his voice remnants of the great traditions of shabad kirtan that was once alive at Gurdwara Janam Asathan Sri Nankana Sahib. I request all the genuine lovers of gurmat sangeet to listen to Bhai Prithipal Singh's shabad kirtan. In some very small pieces, he has given glimpses of his mastery over this dying art.

Bhai Prithipal Singh and Bhai Mohan Pal Singh are not alive anymore, both having passed away before even turning 60. They both lived and died in poverty. Our community never recognised their talents. Yet, they never abandoned their traditions and never compromised with their music. That, I think, is the sign of a true musician.

Mohal Pal Singh is second from left and Prithipal Singh is fifth from the left

13

Bhai Dilbagh Singh and Gulbagh Singh

Pure Classical Musicians

Bhai Dilbagh Singh and Gulbagh Singh belong to a pure rababi kirtania gharana of village Bodal (Bodalan) in Hoshiarpur district of the Bist Doab region of Punjab. The most prominent son of this village was the legendry Dr Mohinder Singh Randhawa (ICS), who was known for his honest and innovative approach and was an extremely efficient senior government official. The forefathers of Bhai Dilbagh Singh and Gulbagh Singh were rababi Muslims and had been musicians for centuries. Their maternal parents were musicians. Several of their near and dear relatives were also hereditary musicians. This was the first generation to become practising Sikhs and regular kirtanias.

The eldest of the four brothers was Bhai Dilbagh Singh. He was born in 1946 in village Bodal itself. He was the head of the jatha. The original raagi jatha consisted of Bhai Dilbagh Singh, Gulbagh Singh, and Iqbal Singh. The fourth and youngest brother is Bhai Davinder Singh, who is also a highly talented musician trained by Ustad Salamat Ali Khan and Nazaqat Ali Khan, formerly of Sham Churasi district Hoshiarpur, who later settled in Pakistan.

Bhai Dilbagh Singh received his initiation into classical music by his grandfather, Bhai Ditta ji, who was an adept classical singer in his own right. His other childhood tutor was his maternal grandfather, Bhai Nand ji. Bhai Nand ji was quite well known in the area. They belonged to the ancient Hoshiarpur School of music, which predates the rise of Patiala Gharana. Bhai Dilbagh Singh's training was fine-tuned by Pandit Babu Ram of Garh-Shanker, who was a very strict disciplinarian teacher. It was very difficult to follow his rigid training regime.

By 1970, Bhai Dilbagh Singh had become an accomplished khayal singer. He was the one who took pains to train his younger brother, Bhai Gulbagh Singh, as his accompanying singer. Both became accomplished harmonium and surmandal players. Their fame reached the SGPC too and the SGPC started inviting them to their classical kirtan darbars. On the birth anniversary of Sri Guru Ram Das in 1974, the most accomplished raagis were given the assignment to perform shabad gayan in Raaga Kedara. There were 42 raagis in total. Bhai Dilbagh Singh and Gulbagh Singh's rendition was a breed apart from the rest of the top musicians and was adjudged the winner. They were especially honoured with the title of Shiromani Kirtanias for the very first time in life. From then on, they began to get noticed more by the lovers of classical music.

Once in 1980, Bhai Dilbagh Singh and Gulbagh Singh were on a tour of Delhi. Ustad Hafeez Ahmed Khan, the head of the classical music department at All India Radio Delhi, the flagship station of All India Radio, was driving by Gurdwara Sri Bangla Sahib in New Delhi when they were performing shabad kirtan in their typical style. He liked their voices and the mastery over music. He was with Sardar Baldev Singh, a great lover of good music. So soulful was the music that they stopped the car and went in. After Bhai

Dilbagh Singh and Gulbagh Singh had finished their chowki of shabad kirtan, Ustad Hafeez Ahmed Khan sent a message to see them. When they came out, he asked them if they were approved radio artists. To this Bhai Dilbagh Singh said, 'We are carefree people. We are not even interested in becoming radio artists.' Despite this, Ustad Hafeez Khan told them that All India Radio Jalandhar would contact them at their village address. Soon after, without even undergoing a formal audition, All India Radio Jalandhar gave them the status of an A-grade artist. This is how they became radio artists and started singing classical music at All India Radio Jalandhar. They also received invitations to sing at the other capital radio stations of India.

By 1982, organisers like Ashwani Kumar, retired I.G. Police, for the Baba Harivallabh Annual Sangeet Sammelan in Jalandhar, noticed their talent. On one wintery day, Bhai Dilbagh Singh received an invitation to perform khayal at the *sammelan.*[68]

The third member of the jatha was Bhai Iqbal Singh, who is also a highly accomplished tabla player. He first learnt tabla-playing from his elder brother, Bhai Dilbagh Singh, and later specialised in it further under the guidance of Bhai Nihal Singh, a second-generation shagird of Bhai Nasira of the Golden Temple.

During the mid-1980s, they toured the other Indian states. In around 1988, they won the title of Sangeet Churamani from the knowledgeable audience of Bhopal, the capital of Madhya Pradesh. For many years, the SGPC in Amritsar has been holding a classical kirtan darbar on the birth anniversary of the fourth master, Sri Guru Ram Das, in October each year. Bhai Dilbagh Singh and Gurbagh Singh were not only invited every year to this programme but were honoured as well.

---

[68] Gathering.

All India Radio did not treat them just as the classical kirtanias, but as some of the finest exponents of khayal, thumri and dadra. Most Sikh religious musicians are kirtanias first and classical musicians later, but in the case of Bhai Dilbagh Singh and Gulbagh Singh, they were classical musicians first and kirtanias later. Even their accreditation at All India Radio classified them as classical musicians.

This duo had learnt the techniques of rendition of ghazal in the classical mode. Since most their life was spent in their native village, their source of livelihood had always been the performance of shabad kirtan in the cluster of villages located close by. They made several recordings of shabad kirtan at the All India Radio Jalandhar. Since their tours of foreign countries had not been too many, they were always hand-to-mouth.

In the early 1980s, they toured Canada and stayed mostly in the province of British Columbia. They approached me to arrange an American visa for them. I tried through Mr Tejinder Singh Kahlon, the then President of the Sikh Cultural Society in the Richmond Hill section of the Borough of Queens in New York City. However, despite our best efforts, their visa was rejected because they did not apply for an American visa in the country of their citizenship. The next time, thus, we sent the sponsorship in India and the visa was granted without a hassle. When they came to New York we hosted them in New Jersey too. Their tour was highly successful and financially rewarding.

From then on, their foreign tours increased, and they developed their own fan-following. On some tours, their youngest brother, Davinder Singh, also joined them. He is indeed a hidden treasure. One of the biggest promoters of musicians in the Toronto area of Canada was Mr Iqbal Singh Mahal, a great fan of Bhai Dilbagh Singh and Gulbagh Singh's music. He always made sure that they got bookings done at the homes of knowledgeable listeners. They were in great demand in the New York area too. In one of their interviews, Iqbal Mahal asked a question, as to which raagi other than their own jatha met with their standards. Bhai Gulbagh Singh answered, 'We like only the raagi jatha of Bhai Dharam Singh Zakhmi (particularly Bhai Shamsher Singh) and that of Bhai Balbir Singh of Tarn Taran (he is the same raagi who was the senior-most musician at the Golden Temple who died on 23 February 2020 due to age-related complications).'

The languages department of Punjab conferred the title of Shiromani Raagis on the duo.

Would you believe that these great musicians were very good players of football too? I have seen them playing football in the parking area of Gurdwara Bridgewater!

In October of 2006, Bhai Dilbagh Singh died of a sudden heart attack. After that the group got disbanded. Bhai Gulbagh Singh is alive and in good health. He lives in the Punjabi agriculturist belt in California, in the Bakers Field area. The third member of the jatha, Bhai Iqbal Singh, teaches tabla at the Khalsa School in Gurdwara Richmond Hill.

Bhai Dilbagh Singh and Gulbagh Singh

14

Bhai Nirmal Singh Khalsa

A God-gifted Musician

Bhai Nirmal Singh Khalsa was a no-holds-barred critic of the selection system of musicians in the Golden Temple and the other shrines governed by the SGPC. The write-up about him will be incomplete without recording what he said in a multitude of interviews, throughout his highly eventful life. He was firm like a rock on what he believed in and was afraid only of the Guru. He was born in a marginal-farming family displaced from Pakistan during the division of Punjab in 1947. The family owned about 50 acres of agricultural land in Chak Number 97 in district Montgomery of West (Pakistani) Punjab.

After their forced exodus into India, for which the family took the Suleimanki Headworks route from district Montgomery to Fazilka Tehsil in Ferozepore district, the family was made to shuttle several times between Jullundur and Ferozepore districts to get some compensatory land allotted for barebones subsistence. Finally, they were allotted some land in a small village near Lohian in Shahkot tehsil of Jullundur district. According to the formula under which they were allotted land in East Punjab, they were supposed to get less than one-third of the land that they had owned in Pakistan, because Indian Punjab did not have enough land left behind by the Muslim landowners when they migrated to Pakistan for the allotment of land to the displaced families from Pakistan. This meant about 17 acres were allotted for a family of six brothers. Actually, his father got about three acres. So, for all practical purposes, his father had to barely subsist on a tiny piece of agricultural land, and they had nothing else to fall back on.

Born on 12 April 1952 in a village called Jandwala Bhimeshah near Ferozepore, in the home of his maternal grandparents, young Nirmal Singh went to the village school near Lohian Khas, which was a primary school. Bhai Nirmal Singh passed the fifth class and then started helping his father. His village had access to a bulky wood cabinet radio receiver, provided by the Punjab Government, to keep the village folks informed about the latest agricultural research undertaken by the College of Agriculture, Ludhiana, and Khalsa College (Agriculture), Amritsar.

Rather than tuning in to the agricultural announcements from All India Radio Jalandhar, young Nirmal Singh became fond of listening to a Punjabi program called Punjabi Darbar from Radio Pakistan Lahore in the evenings. It used to play some shabads rendered by one rababi Muslim musician who was formerly from Amritsar. His radio name was Bhai Lal, but he was not the real legendry Bhai Lal of the Golden Temple who hailed from another musical family. This musician's real name was Aashik Ali, and he used to sing qawwalis and qaats in Lahore for a living. At the request of the authorities of Radio Pakistan Lahore, this musician refreshed his knowledge of gurbani to record some shabads for the popular program Punjabi Darbar that beamed to the Indian Punjab. Bhai Lal also used to perform shabad kirtan on Guru Nanak Parkash Gurpurb at Gurdwara Janam Asthan Sri Nankana Sahib, on the martyrdom Gurpurb of Guru Arjan Dev ji in Gurdwara Dera Sahib in Lahore, and on Baisakhi at Gurdwara Sri Panja Sahib Hassan Abdal in the remote west of the Punjab province. Young Nirmal Singh developed a liking for Bhai Lal Junior's style of music too. Child Nirmal Singh also developed taste for the magical voices of Pakistan's popular vocal maestros like Mehdi Hassan, Pervez Mehdi, Ghulam Ali, and Showqat Ali.

As he entered the rebellious teens, his love for classical and semi-classical music became a difficult-to-suppress obsession. He had absolutely no knowledge of the raagas they sang in, but he could appreciate the sophisticated music, nevertheless. Among Pakistan's leading female artists, he liked Roshan Ara Begum, Noorjehan, Iqbal Bano and Farida Khanum to name a few.

His father was tough to deal with and whimsical in nature, but his mother was considerate and sympathetic to her son's aspirations. One day, he discussed his plans with her, and told her that he would not want to continue toiling in the fields and attending to the family's herd of cattle. He bluntly expressed his desire to become a religious musician. His mother was willing to risk some savings to let her son explore the avenue of religious music in an unknown city.

One of his uncles, Bhai Gurbachan Singh, was a driver of the then President of SGPC, Sant Channan Singh, and later, he drove Shiromani Akali Dal President Sant Fateh Singh's car too. At one time he drove Sant Chanan Singh's successor, Jathedar Gurcharan Singh Tohra's, car as well. Bhai Gurbachan Singh was a trained classical kirtania too and he served the raagi jatha of Bhai Gurmel Singh of the Golden Temple. On the hesitant suggestion of Bhai Gurbachan Singh and Nirmal Singh's mother consent, young Nirmal Singh packed up for Amritsar. The bus fare was about one rupee. In Amritsar he reached the Golden Temple and met his uncle, Bhai Gurbachan Singh, to talk about his firm desire of becoming a religious musician. Bhai Gurbachan Singh reluctantly talked to the president of SGPC Jathedar, Gurcharan Singh Tohra, to get young Nirmal Singh admitted to Shaheed Sikh Missionary College in Putlighar near Khalsa College, Amritsar. It appeared to be an uphill task.

Nirmal Singh's level of education was too low, he had barely passed primary school, and the interview was conducted by a high-powered committee consisting of the SGPC President Jathedar Gurcharan Singh Tohra, Principal Harbhajan Singh, Ustad Avtar Singh Naaz, and Sardar Jodh Singh of All India Radio Jalandhar. They asked him to sing a shabad, which he did not know. Rather he sang a religious poem on the supreme sacrifice of the Sahibzadas of the tenth master, Guru Gobind Singh ji. The selectors laughed heartily at his ignorance about gurbani, but disregarding his complete lack of knowledge about the real gurbani, they noticed a sweet melodious voice in the young aspirant. Contrary to expectations, he was selected as a student of Sikh religious music in the Sikh Missionary College, Putli Ghar, Amritsar. From 1974 to 1976, for three years, he was put to a rigorous training regime in music under a brilliant teacher of music, Bhai Avtar Singh Naaz, and was awarded a diploma.

His first important posting was as a teacher of music at the gurmat college in Rishikesh (Uttar Pradesh) in 1977, where he trained a lot of children from needy families in gurmat sangeet. In the very next year 1978, his second posting was made 300 miles away at Buddha Johar in Sriganganagar district in Rajasthan as a teacher at the Shaheed Sikh Missionary College. He stayed there for a year but made several important connections, which served him well in later years.

His wish was to become a hazoori raagi at Sri Darbar Sahib in Amritsar. Finally, in 1979, the SGPC posted him as a supporting musician with a senior lead musician, Bhai Gurmej Singh. Bhai Gurmej Singh was a very experienced old-fashioned musician. He guided Bhai Nirmal Singh on where to pause and be soft and where to lay stress. Bhai Gurmej Singh discovered in young Nirmal Singh a quick learner.

In 1984, during Operation Blue Star, Bhai Nirmal Singh was on duty at the Golden Temple. Due to intermittent firing, he could not perform his duty as a musician but witnessed the notorious operation from start to finish. His narration was frank and immersed in emotions but like a trained parrot. He saw the most heinous part of the operation. The operation started with a big bang. A deafening cannon fire at about 4 a.m. on 3 June shattered the silence of the pre-dawn in Amritsar. The obvious intention was to blow up the overhead potable water tank, which supplied water to the entire Golden Temple complex. As intended, the concrete tank came down in a pile of debris. The surrounding areas were inundated with water. There were some trained fighters of Dal Khalsa on top of the tank. They probably had some intuition and came down prior to the canon burst. Due to poor intelligence some shots that were meant to be fired at the Akal Takhat were fired on the Darshani Deohri causing some damage. A couple of battle tanks entered the *parikrama*[69] through the langar-side entrance gate. The marble steps of the entrance were badly damaged. These tanks did a lot of damage to the Sri Akal Takhat Sahib. The massive operation came to an end on 6 June 1984. Bhai Nirmal Singh could not move from his hideout for a long time. Stinking dead bodies were strewn all around the parikrama.

Though shaken badly by nightmarish memories, Bhai Nirmal Singh picked up courage and started his riyaz of classical music once again. Senior iconic musicians like Bhai Balbir Singh and Bhai Bakhshish Singh started appreciating his hard work and perseverance. Even Bhai Gurmel Singh and Bhai Gurmej Singh were all praise for his perseverance. His uncle, Bhai Gurbachan Singh, was the assistant to Bhai Gurmel Singh. He was Bhai Nirmal Singh's greatest well-wisher.

In 1986, when some vacancies for the musicians opened at the Golden Temple, he was allowed to form his own kirtania jatha. His first choice was of Kanwaljit Singh, but the association lasted for a very short duration. Then he chose Bhai Darshan Singh as the second vocal musician with harmonium as the

---

[69] The perimeter path around the sacred *sarovar* of the Golden Temple where devotees ritually move clockwise in reverence.

instrument and Bhai Kartar Singh as a drummer (tabla player). This jatha continued unaltered for 34 years.

Bhai Nirmal Singh was a witness to yet another police and para-military action at the Golden Temple complex. It happened during 1986 itself on 30 April. According to his own narration, Bhai Nirmal Singh Khalsa was on regular kirtan duty. Normally the slot used to be for an hour and a half, but no raagi jatha came to relieve him. So, he kept performing his duty. His marathon kirtan slot lasted nine hours. He was hungry and needed to clear his bladder. At the end of nine hours, he requested the on-duty ardasia to perform the ardas. While moving out of the sanctum sanctorum, he had to crawl to reach a place, where he could urinate. He was caught and arrested by the para-military forces. He bravely explained his position. There was one deputy inspector general of police of the Central Reserve Police force, Mr Chaman Lal perhaps. He quickly understood Bhai Nirmal Singh's predicament and asked his staff to escort him and drop him off at his village near Lohian Khas in Jalandhar district. Surprisingly, after the instructions from a superior, the police treated him with due respect.

Bhai Nirmal Singh kept polishing his singing skills by regular riyaz of the raagas that he was supposed to sing. One day, on one of his many trips to the USA, perhaps in 1990 or 1991, I was driving Bhai Nirmal Singh to a gurdwara in New Jersey. In my car, I had cassette tapes of the choicest Sikh music. Out of all the tapes, I chose a special one in the voice of M.S. Subhalakshmi of Madras (now Chennai). As it unfolded, Bhai Sahib started saying, 'Wah, what a beautiful voice'. When the tape ended, Bhai Nirmal Singh asked me as to whose voice it was. I told him, it was M.S. Subhalakshmi, the finest Karnataka classical musician of Southern India. He told me that other than Bhai Santa Singh, this is the finest rendition that he had heard in his life. He was a great admirer of Bhai Samund Singh, Sant Sujan Singh, and Bhai Mohan Pal Singh too.

Bhai Nirmal Singh loved the voice of the ghazal singer Ghulam Ali of Pakistan, and he nursed a strong desire to be his shagird. One day, on a tour of the United Kingdom, he heard that Ghulam Ali was also in England. Bhai Nirmal Singh made a trip to London to see his idol. When they actually met, he discovered, to his great surprise, that even Ghulam Ali was listening to him! Bhai Nirmal Singh expressed his desire to become his disciple to which Ghulam Ali consented. From then on Bhai Nirmal Singh started mastering Ghulam Ali's style. Sometimes Ghulam Ali visited him in Amritsar, and he learnt the finer points of Ghulam Ali's classical renditions. At one time his style became the carbon copy of Ghulam Ali's style of ghazal music, but as he started developing his distinct style based on gurmat sangeet, he received a panth-wide name and fame. His voice was a vibrant and powerful one. He even reached newer heights in the paath of Sri Japji Sahib and Rehras Sahib. If one listens to his nitnem, it is an altogether great feeling.

Over the years, Bhai Nirmal Singh had cultured his voice so well that the most knowledgeable listeners started calling him an ustad musician. He became the favourite of most of the staff associated with music at all the stations of All India Radio in Punjab. All India Radio Jalandhar conferred on him the title of an A-class singer and made a lot of his recordings. Bhai Jwala Singh had imbibed the ancient dhrupad and dhamar style of music. Bhai Santa Singh was the king of reet and Sant Sujan Singh had excelled in the qawwali style of music. By the same yardstick, Bhai Nirmal Singh became synonymous with the ghazal style of music, but his variety of tunes was so vast that it can be presumed that he had developed his exclusive brand of music.

In 2009, the then President of India, Mrs Pratibha Singh Patil, conferred on him the coveted Padma Shri award. The then Prime Minister of India, Dr Manmohan Singh, and his wife, Mrs Gursharan Kaur were fond of listening to his music. Mrs Gursharan Kaur is a known lover of gurbani kirtan since her childhood. She became fond of listening to Bhai Nirmal Singh's rendition of 'Asa Di Vaar' and her husband listened to his shabad kirtan before going to bed. It was revealed by Bhai Nirmal Singh that in all probability he had got the Padma Shri award due to the personal efforts of Prime Minister, Dr Manmohan Singh. Normally such national-level awards are recommended by the Governments of the states of domicile of the proficient artists. Actually, in the case of music, a high-powered committee of experts sits down, listens to the music of the person recommended and then decides after a long process of deliberations. Bhai Nirmal Singh had indeed cultured his voice so much, that even his ordinary renditions got the status of a landmark. His voice was independent of his age and kept improving year after year. Even the film industry of India liked his resonating vibrant voice. India's reputed music director, Sardar Uttam Singh, used his voice in the film *Nanak Shah Faqir*. Bhai Nirmal Singh rendered the aarti most professionally for this off-beat film.

Bhai Nirmal Singh visited almost 70 countries of the world. Most of these included European and North American countries. He was a great lover of the environment. Many times, he met Sant Balbir Singh Seechewal and appreciated his efforts to clean the Kali Vein in Sultanpur Lodhi. His own village was located very close to Sultanpur Lodhi near Lohian Khas. Bhai Nirmal Singh Khalsa had the distinction of performing shabad kirtan at all five Sikh religious takhats.

He was on the selection committee of musicians of the SGPC where he always preferred to take a strong stand in favour of the most meritorious candidates. He was an outspoken critic of wrong things. One day Ghulam Ali asked him to take him to the Golden Temple. On entering the premises, he heard an untrained voice performing shabad kirtan at the Golden Temple. Ghulam Ali was shocked to hear a raw, untrained voice at a place known for its excellence in music. He remarked that once upon a time this place was the source of music even for the film industry of India and now the standard his gone down drastically. Here I am pointing out that one of India's pioneer music directors, Master Ghulam Haider, was the son of a rababi Muslim musician of the Golden Temple. So was another ace music composer Rashid Attre. Sain Akhtar Hussain was the son of another rababi musician of the Golden Temple. A popular music director of Bombay, S. Mohinder, learnt classical music from Bhai

Samund Singh, a top musician of Gurdwara Janam Asthan Sri Nankana Sahib. Vinod learnt music by listening to the rababi musicians of Gurdwara Dera Sahib Lahore. Master Hans Raj Behl was under the influence of Sikh religious music. Music director, Shyam Sunder was deeply influenced by the music of the Golden Temple. The list is long and never-ending.

Bhai Nirmal Singh Khalsa has been one of the most professionally recorded Sikh religious musicians ever. According to YouTube statistics, some of his most popular numbers include complete 'Asa Di Vaar', Aarti, Japji Sahib, Rehras Sahib, Sukhmani Sahib. The popular, available on YouTube, shabads include:

Kar Bande Tu Bandagi

Sajjan Mere Rangle

Eh doye Naina Mat Chhoyo

Sun Yaar Hamare Sajjan

Babiha Amrit Vele Bolya

Beet Jaahe Janam

Raag Basant

Bighan Na Kou Laage

Kaali Koyal Tu Kit Gun Kaali

Koi Bole Raam Raam

Mauli Dharti Maulya Akash

Too Daryao Daana Beena

Dhan Dhan Ramdas Gur

Birkhey Heith Sab Jant

Jiska Sahib Dahda Hoye

Har Kirtan Suniye

Jaisi Main Aaweh Khasam Ki Baani

Tum Daate Thaker Pritpalak

Jog Baniya Tera Kirtan Gaayi

Rain Gayi Mat Din Bhi Jaaye

Prem Laago Har

Gun Gobind Gaayo Nahin

Prabh Harimandir

Dukh Na Paave Koi

More Babihe Bolde

There are possibly more renditions of shabads in his sweet and melodious voice, including All India Radio recordings, but mentioning every rendition is not possible. He admitted to remembering at least 500 shabads of gurbani by heart and he was capable of singing each one effortlessly. Towards his last few years, he was not serving the SGPC.

Bhai Nirmal Singh Khalsa had seasoned his voice so well over decades that he was capable of rendering gurmat sangeet for at least two more decades, but, as the saying goes, 'What man proposes; God disposes'. The Lord wanted something else – at a time when his demand was at its peak, his life was cut short by Coronavirus and a heart ailment. He was most in demand during the 550th birth anniversary of Sri Guru Nanak Dev ji. After 12 November 2019, he went to the

USA to fulfil his commitments. He came back to India soon thereafter.

On 20 and 21 March 2020, he had some programs in Chandigarh. Soon thereafter he returned to his base in Amritsar. He had a minor cold while in Chandigarh. In Amritsar his condition did not improve, rather it worsened. He got checked in Guru Ram Das University of Medical Sciences in Amritsar. However, some confusion led to his transfer to Guru Nanak (Civil) Hospital attached to the Government Medical College Amritsar. In this hospital, his condition worsened even further. He was feeling restless on 1 April and on 2 April and at around 4:30 a.m. he passed away.

The news of his death due to Covid spread like a wildfire. The Government and his family wanted to cremate his mortal remains without much delay. They tried to cremate him in Sultanwind, Gurdwara Shahidan Cremation Ground and at the Durgiana Temple Cremation Ground, but all of them refused. Then they approached the people of Verka for cremation in their village cremation area, but even the people of Verka refused the cremation, primarily in fear of getting Coronavirus. Finally, at 9:30 p.m., he was cremated. The land was made available by the people of Verka on more than one acre of common land in another village.

Bhai Nirmal Singh received a lot of respect while living. Even the SGPC conferred on him the honour of Shiromani Raagi. However, in death, he received only humiliation. While alive he worked hard and served the community to the best of his ability. In his untimely death, we owe him a lot.

The Bhog of Sri Akhand Paath Sahib was performed jointly by the SGPC and his bereaved family on 19 April 2020 (Sunday) at the Gurdwara Kaulsar in Amritsar. Due to Coronavirus related restrictions, only a handful of people were invited. Vairagmayi kirtan was performed by a blind hazoori raagi, Bhai Lakhwinder Singh. The Government of Punjab sent its message of condolence. The President of the Shiromani Akali Dal also sent a message of condolence. His portrait will be installed in the Central Sikh Museum in Sri Darbar Sahib. There is also talk of building a suitable memorial for him, but only time will tell what the Government and the SGPC will do for him.

My own suggestion is that the museum to be constructed in Bhai Nirmal Singh Khalsa's memory should include the music of scores of other Sikh religious musicians of substance as well. Some experts of music should be consulted to decide the contents of this museum.

15

Dr Jagir Singh

A Melodious Singer

Dr Jagir Singh is the eldest of the three illustrious sons of the accomplished kirtania, Bhai Uttam Singh Patang. All three are academically brilliant men, and all are holders of M.A. PhD degrees. The youngest of the three, Gurnam Singh, was still pursuing his education.

Their ancestry belongs to district Gujrat in the Rawalpindi division of West (Pakistani) Punjab. Their ancestral spoken dialect, according to my research, is Standard (Central) Punjabi of the Lahore division. On one side of Gujrat is the district of Gujranwala of Lahore division, the home district of Emperor Ranjit Singh, and on the other side is district Jhelum of Rawalpindi division. The most famous musician of Gujrat was the Punjabi folk and Urdu ghazal singer, Showqat Ali.

The communal strife associated with

the independence of India and the ill-fated division of Punjab forced their ancestors to abandon their homes and hearths in what is now Pakistan and move to East (Indian) Punjab. They settled in a village in the Rajpura sub-division of the Patiala district. After two years, on 4 October 1949, Jagir Singh was born. His original education took place in rural Patiala. His father joined the service of Shiromani Gurdwara Prabandhak Committee as a kirtania and served in Patiala and Fatehgarh Sahib as a well-respected hazoori raagi.

He did his master's degree from Punjabi University in Patiala as a private student in 1972. As for music, Dr Jagir Singh was initiated into gurmat sangeet by his father. Since his childhood, he had developed a special taste for it. His voice is naturally melodious.

True to his inclination, he enrolled himself as a student of PhD in the subject of gurmat sangeet's relationship with the Sikh holy scriptures in Panjab University in Chandigarh under the esteemed guidance of Professor Dr Surinder Singh Kohli in 1976. He completed his PhD in 1980. From 1974 to 1976, he served as a lecturer in the Guru Gobind Singh College in Chandigarh. Prior to doing his master's degree, from 1968 to 1971, he served in the raagi jatha of the iconic musician, Bhai Bakhshish Singh, who was then the most popular kirtania in Patiala. Assisting a highly accomplished musician comes with its own advantages and Jagir Singh imbibed those. After leaving Bhai Bakhshish Singh's group, he became an unattached freelance kirtania. He learnt the finest points of classical music from Pandit Yashpal, who had settled in Chandigarh then. As a freelancer, his younger brother, Bachittar Singh joined his raagi jatha.

In 1976, he left the service of Sri Guru Gobind Singh College in Chandigarh and joined the Punjab State School Education Board in Mohali as a subject expert associated with the Punjabi language. He served in this capacity up to

2003 and then became the deputy director, where he served from 2003 to 2005. He received more seniority between 2005 and 2007. In 2009, after retirement from the school education board, he joined the Punjabi University in Patiala as the head of the Gurmat Sangeet Department, where he stayed for one year. He enjoyed his position thoroughly while serving the Punjab School Education Board. During this period, he made two highly successful trips to the United States of America. His music was extensively recorded on the finest Dolby recording system in the USA. He also became a B-high grade artist as a religious musician at All India Radio Jalandhar.

Like the King of Ghazals, Talat Mahmood, Dr Jagir Singh's voice is also sweet as velvet. It was his voice that made his raagi jatha so popular amongst the elite Sikh bureaucracy based in Chandigarh. Most of the best-known raagis were already settled in the big urban agglomerations of Delhi, Patiala, Ludhiana, Jalandhar and Amritsar. Though it was the fast-growing capital of Punjab, Chandigarh was considered a small city and most of the well-known raagis were unprepared to settle in this untried city. Professor Jagir Singh's emergence on the scene was a windfall for Chandigarh and the knowledgeable residents of the city welcomed him with open arms.

The first time I met him was during a thanksgiving kirtan held at the residence of Sardar Kartar Singh Mann, special secretary to the Punjab Chief Minister, Giani Zail Singh, in 1973. I was thoroughly impressed by the sweet and flexible voices of Professor Jagir Singh and his brother, Bachittar Singh. They enthralled the audience with profound music for over an hour. Their style of rendition made me inquisitive and I engaged them in a conversation for a good one hour after the programme had ended. They told me that they hated those raagis who blindly copied Bollywood music.

They felt that Bollywood music takes one away from spirituality. This is what they told me – if a song is picturised on Nargis, Meena Kumari, or Madhubala, the listener will think about those glamorous ladies rather than focusing on the music or the lyrics of the song. Therefore, Dr Jagir Singh always preferred to create his own tunes, which were inspired by the raagas contained in Sri Guru Granth Sahib or the other raagas and raagnis similar to those. This novel concept of composing tunes touched my heart, and I became their lifelong admirer.

I also heard his shabad kirtan at the residences of several other high ranking government officers, industrialists and common folks. His appearances at All India Radio Jalandhar with Bhai Bakhshish Singh also made his voice more familiar to me and others.

I lost my father on 31 August 1976 which really shook me up. At his funeral, Professor Jagir Singh and Bachittar Singh performed shabad kirtan. My mother was quite impressed, and she wanted to hire his services for my father's antim ardas too. I wanted to invite Bhai Mohan Pal Singh and a party from Patiala, the second generation rababi kirtanias of Gurdwara Janam Asthan Sri Nankana Sahib. Bhai Mohan Pal Singh's own voice was very well cultured. In fact, both the jathas came and performed highly emotional kirtan. My father was also fond of good music, so I am satisfied that his last rites reflected his taste.

I moved to the United States in November of 1979. In 1982, I was the secretary of Gurdwara Bridgewater in New Jersey. A very good friend of mine, Mr Arjit Singh Mahal, was scheduled to visit his ageing parents residing in Sector 11 of Chandigarh. He was looking for a good musician to perform shabad kirtan at his parents' house. I suggested the name of Dr Jagir Singh. He wanted the kirtan to be performed in ancient tunes accompanied by string and bow instruments. For that, I suggested the name of an accomplished sarangi player, Janab Ismael Bechain, who hailed from Uttar Pradesh but was living in Chandigarh. The recording happened beautifully. When he returned to the USA, he recommended that Dr Jagir Singh's jatha be sent a sponsorship to perform kirtan in the USA.

I hurriedly composed the letter of sponsorship and posted it to the American Embassy in New Delhi. At first, the over-worked American Embassy became suspicious about his presumed intentions of settling in America and they refused to grant him the visa, but a thoroughly angry Arjit Singh Mahal visited India again and successfully argued with the officials of the Embassy to grant him a visitor's visa for six months in 1983. Mr Mohinder Singh Puar was the President of Gurdwara Bridgewater and Mr Mohinder Singh Bathala was the Secretary. They both cooperated very well and accorded well-deserved respect to Dr Jagir Singh. We arranged his kirtans in the other gurdwaras in the neighbouring states too, including the largest gurdwara, the Gurudwara Richmond Hill New York, which had knowledgeable listeners.

True to our commitment to the Embassy, Dr Jagir Singh returned to India well before the expiry date of his visa. His first visa was for him alone. Since he did not travel with his full party, he took with him an electronic tanpura, and for some recordings, tabla accompaniment. He also took some cassettes with recordings of his favourite taals including kehrwa, dadra, teental, ek taal, jhap taal and the like. Being well educated, he was well prepared for all eventualities, but wherever it was possible, we arranged the tabla accompaniment for him. It was our wish to treat him as a family member, show him more parts of the USA and let him feel fully at home. I was asked by the organisers of a summer vacation camp in the Pittsburgh area to teach Sikh history to American-born Sikh children in a special camp in rural Pennsylvania. My batch-mate from the engineering course, Er. Jarnail Singh Ghumman was overall in-charge of the camp. I offered to take Dr Jagir Singh along to teach shabad kirtan to the kids, which they readily agreed to. I drove him all the way from New Jersey in my own car. It gave me immense pleasure to see him enjoy the scenery on the way.

He used his skills as a college lecturer to make the learning of kirtan easy and interesting for the kids. For about a fortnight, he stayed in the camp as a family member and an 'uncle' for the kids. For days after he had returned from the camp, we kept receiving calls from the parents of kids.

He recorded the complete path of the Sri Guru Granth Sahib in 36 cassettes and these tapes began selling like hotcakes as there were many Sindhis who had settled all over the USA and they began buying these.

The second time he received the visa for visiting the USA was in 1985, when once again I was the secretary of Gurdwara Bridgewater in New Jersey and a highly cooperative Er. Harbir Singh Jawanda was the President. This time the attitude of the American Embassy was friendlier and the full group of three musicians received the visa without any hassle. His brother, Bachittar Singh, was also a part of the group. Both brothers did very well and received a lot of ovations from the knowledgeable audience. Within a month, however, Bachittar Singh, who was outside India for the first time and had a less than a year-old son in India, began feeling homesick. Hence, suddenly, he packed his bag and left for India! Again, Dr Jagir Singh had an incomplete jatha. So, we arranged temporary side singers for him, all of whom benefited from his education. This time he explained the meaning of the baani to the audience.

In his spare time, he listened to the great masters like

Ustad Bade Ghulam Ali Khan, Ustad Ameer Khan, Ustad Abdul Qareem Khan, Dagar Brothers, Pandit Bhim Sen Joshi, Pandit Jasraj and Bhai Samund Singh.

Dr Jagir Singh was formally recognised for his extraordinary services to gurmat sangeet by the Punjab Government during the height of the insurgency in 1989 and was bestowed with the title of Shiromani Kirtania. Because of his sweet voice and fine manners, the graph of his popularity rose even in the worst of times.

On the morning of 18 December 2001, he was travelling in his car from Chandigarh to Amritsar to deliver a lecture on Gurbani Kirtan in a college. It was a foggy morning and at about 7 a.m., all of a sudden, a thick patch of heavy fog appeared. The road from Ropar to Phagwara was not doubled yet and his car was crushed by a bus coming from the other side. Seeing the condition of the car, no one would believe that the occupant could survive, but God saved him! He was hospitalised for months, underwent several operations, but miraculously survived. His spinal cord was saved, but after that accident, he was unable to perform shabad kirtan anymore with folded legs in the presence of the Sri Guru Granth Sahib. However, honours kept pouring in afterwards too. In 2003, he was chosen for the prestigious New Delhi based Sangeet Natak Academy Award. Currently, although he is mentally still quite active, he has given up public performances of kirtan.

16

Giani Obaidullah

It was sometime in the mid-1960s in Chandigarh, I was fiddling with our 1930s old family radio when, suddenly, I discovered high-quality Indian film and non-film music being played without any announcement. The wavelength was approximately 475 meters. There was no news broadcast also, just non-stop Indian music. I got hooked on it and began listening to this mysterious radio station every evening. Then one day came an announcement in chaste Urdu that this was Radio Pakistan Lahore doing test transmissions. After that news broadcasts in Urdu, English and Punjabi also got aired.

Post this I could listen, for the first time, to a special program in Punjabi. It had shabads rendered mostly by Bhai Lal Rababi Junior, formerly of Amritsar, but at that time living in Lahore. Some news from the Indian Punjab also was read in Punjabi. There was a program of commentaries on news and a religious speech about the Sikh history, Sikh philosophy and similarities in Muslim and Sikh religious beliefs. It was called the *Punjabi Darbar*. Obviously, it was a program that had been sponsored by the Ministry of External Affairs of Pakistan to mellow down the tense relations between the Muslims and Sikhs born out of the communal riots of 1947.

The in-charge of this program was Giani Obaidullah, who spoke sophisticated Punjabi. He was assisted by another individual – Giani Hari Singh. He was the head priest of Gurdwara Janam Asthan Sri Nankana Sahib. On need-based assignments, he was made to shuttle to Gurdwara Dera Sahib Lahore and Gurdwara Sri Panja Sahib in Hassanabdal.

In May-June of 1970, I visited Lahore, along with my parents, as a part of the Shiromani Gurdwara Prabandhak Committee Amritsar's official jatha that had been sent to Pakistan for observing the Martyrdom Gurpurb of the fifth Guru, Sri Guru Arjan Dev ji, in Gurdwara Dera Sahib Lahore. We did not cross over from the Attari/Wagha check post, because during the 1965 Indo-Pakistan War, Pakistan's infrastructure at the Wagha Border was badly damaged and they had requested the opening of trade and passenger traffic at the Hussainiwala/Ganda Singh Wala border crossing in Ferozepore district. So, we went to Kasur by bus and took the old Ferozepore-Lahore Railway line to reach Lahore. In Lahore, we stayed at the Gurdwara Dera Sahib. The next morning, the gurdwara was thoroughly washed to prepare for the akhand paath of the Sri Guru Granth Sahib.

As the akhand paath started, a man, who seemed to be in his late 50s, was seen coming. He was carrying a big spool-type tape recorder. He opened it, loaded a tape on it and started recording interviews with the visitors. My father was one of the first to be interviewed. I was curious to know about this man. He told me that his name is Obaidullah and that he had come from Radio Pakistan Lahore to cover the annual event. During the question-answer session, we became friends.

He told me that he was taking care of the Punjabi

Darbar program of Radio Pakistan Lahore. During our discussion, he told me of the perils of running a program like Punjabi Darbar. His biggest problem was recording shabads that were to be broadcast in his program. He admitted that the only musician he could rely on was Bhai Lal Junior (his proper name is Aashik Ali and he is formerly from Amritsar). He lamented that he was not getting good musicians from India and added that Bhai Santa Singh died and Bhai Samund Singh was not available. Moreover, he claimed that the SGPC was not sending any good musicians to Pakistan. He was right, but I did not tell him that the SGPC was seriously short of good musicians! On my asking, he told me that out of the Indian Sikh musicians, he liked Professor Sohan Singh of the Agra Gharana and the Singh Bandhus, Tejpal Singh and Surinder Singh. I told him that Bhai Bakhshish Singh was very good too.

By the end of 1979, I came to the United States of America. Since coming to America, I have been visiting India every year, but I have never heard the voice of Giani Obaidullah. I hope he is alive and in good health.

17

Bhai Harjinder Singh Srinagarwale

A Multi-faceted Kirtania

If you type the words shabad kirtan on YouTube, one of the first names that pop up is that of Bhai Harjinder Singh Srinagarwale. This shows the immense popularity of the sweet voice of this musician. He possesses a god-gifted melodious voice.

Bhai Harjinder Singh hails from the Gurdaspur district and was born in 1958 in a Gursikh family of rural Gurdaspur. Since his childhood, he tried to remember gurbani and attempted its rendition in various permutations and combinations of tunes. Obviously, he had some role models, which he does not divulge.

At the age of 17, in 1975, he joined the Damdami Taksal at Chowk Mehta headed by Sant Kartar Singh Bhindranwale in rural Amritsar. This taksal is known for its discipline in learning the proper pronunciation of the recitation of gurbani. There was another famous musician, Principal Baldev Singh on its rolls. Principal Baldev Singh was adequately knowledgeable about gurmat sangeet too. Bhai Harjinder Singh must have learnt the intricacies of most of the raagas written in the Guru Granth Sahib from Principal Baldev Singh. This explains his acquaintance with gurmat sangeet. Officially, his early training in gurmat sangeet was at the Sikh Missionary College, Putli Ghar, Amritsar.

In the spring of 1980, Bhai Harjinder Singh's raagi jatha, then not very well known, reached Srinagar in the Valley of Kashmir. The communal environment was not as badly vitiated then. The audience of Gurdwara Sri Guru Singh Sabha in Srinagar was quite sophisticated, and some tourists enhanced the taste and flavour of the audience. Everyone welcomed the young group of musicians with open arms. The jatha, which hailed from the rural belt of Gurdaspur, easily mingled with the sophisticated audience of Srinagar. Bhai Harjinder Singh learnt a lot from them.

After about two years, he, along with his younger brother, Bhai Maninder Singh, began to stay at Ludhiana in winter and at Srinagar in summer. Slowly, he became famous not only in Kashmir but elsewhere in India too. From 1980, his demand rose a great deal by word of mouth.

With time, his fertile brain started coining newer tunes and he started recording more and more cassette tapes. His preference has generally been light music. In fact, during the cassette tape era, he had about 60 tapes to his credit. Some tapes sold like hotcakes. At one time, a famous and classically well-groomed playback singer of Bollywood, Jaspinder Narula, published some tapes as a part of Bhai Harjinder Singh Srinagarwale's raagi jatha. These tapes became best-selling albums. After that, his demand increased even more all over India.

From 1982, Bhai Harjinder Singh served Gurdwara Sabzi Mandi in Ludhiana for a total of four years. After that, he served Sri Guru Singh Sabha Gurdwara of Ludhiana for another three years. Subsequently, his worldwide engagements became so enormous that he resigned from Ludhiana's largest gurdwara too and started travelling all over India and the world. Bhai Harjinder Singh Srinagarwale is now a widely travelled musician and his favourite country is the USA.

He has performed shabad kirtan in almost every famous gurdwara of India. I wish he had spent a lot of time in the service of the Sikh community's most favoured shrine, the Golden Temple, as well. He would have then been able to imbibe the finest points of gurmat sangeet from Bhai Balbir Singh, the former hazoori raagi of the Golden Temple, just like what Bhai Sarbjeet Singh Laddi did. I have heard a lot of Bhai Harjinder Singh's tapes and CDs. His voice is very sweet, and he has a lot of variation in his vocal cords. One day, I happened to hear one of his classical music CDs. It was much better than the renditions of most of the present-day Sikh musicians.

If I come across him someday, my advice to him will be to listen more and more to the music of Bhai Avtar Singh Gurcharan Singh (formerly of Sultanpur Lodhi and later on of Delhi), Bhai Santa Singh (formerly of the Golden Temple and later of Delhi), Bhai Balbir Singh of the Golden Temple in Amritsar, Bhai Mohan Pal Singh, Bhai Kishan Pal Singh, Bhai Joginder Singh and Mohinder Singh, Bhai Gian Singh Almast, Bhai Jagtar Singh Fakkar, Bhai Dharam Singh Zakhmi, Bhai Piara Singh, and Bhai Bakhshish Singh to name a few. Some of the *namdharis*, like Bhai Baljit Singh, are also brilliant. The result of listening to the great masters will be amazing. These days a lot of their music is available on YouTube also.

Now that he has earned a lot of name and fame, he has a duty towards the community too, which has lost all its most-accomplished musical icons of the twentieth century. He has sung a lot for the masses – now is the time to sing for the classes too. He needs to take a deeper plunge into classical music.

18

Dr Gurnam Singh

A Brilliant Scholar and a Musician

The most famous and brilliant of the three sons of Late Bhai Uttam Singh Patang is his youngest son, Dr Gurnam Singh. Bhai Uttam Singh Patang was an acclaimed hazoori raagi of the SGPC, Amritsar, serving at two closely located historic gurdwaras at Fatehgarh Sahib and Patiala (Dukh Niwaran Sahib).

He was born on 17 April 1959. Being the youngest of the three male siblings, he was very close to his father. Like the elder two, his father wanted the third son also to become

a religious musician. His father used to wake up quite early in the morning to perform 'Asa Di Vaar' well before dawn every day.

Before attaining the age of ten, young Gurnam Singh started learning gurbani and the grammar of classical music. His father initially trained him to play the tabla. At an age when other kids listened to Punjabi folk and Bollywood Hindi music, Gurnam Singh would listen to semi-classical ghazals, thumris, dadras and the other forms of Hindustani classical music. By the age of 11, he became a reasonably good tabla player and often accompanied his father.

Tastes inculcated at a very young age keep developing all through life. So, his interest in music started getting stronger and stronger. In his school days, he started entering competitions for spiritual singing and won some prizes. He also developed a taste for ghazal singing and he became a good ghazal singer. For becoming a ghazal singer, he needed to develop a decent pronunciation of the Urdu language, which he did by learning proper Urdu from experts. His first teachers of music were his father and elder brother, Jagir Singh. Later, he took training from C.M. Dhawan, and then he plunged headlong into gurmat sangeet.

He learnt music from Professor Shamsher Singh Kareer too. For intensive coaching in the grammar of Sikh music, he became a student of the legendry Professor Tara Singh, who authored some books too on ancient Sikh religious music. He began staying in a rented accommodation on Patiala's famous Passi Road, where other musicians of Patiala and its vicinity used to congregate. This place, in fact, became an informal club for lovers of music.

He passed his M.A. in sangeet gayan and then enrolled himself for a PhD at the Delhi University on the topic of *A Musicological Study of Guru Nanak Baani*. He did his doctorate thereafter. At one time he published an album of

Urdu ghazals called *Chand Tanha Hai*. It is still popular with those who have heard it.

For the furtherance of his love for music, he applied for an audition test to become a musician at All India Radio Jalandhar. He passed the test and realised his dream to become a radio singer. As a radio singer, initially, he rendered both ghazals and gurmat sangeet. Some of his most popular recordings of gurmat sangeet were published under the brand name Gavahu Sachi Baani. Dr Kanwaljit Singh, the present head of the Department of Musicology at the Punjabi University accompanied Dr Gurnam Singh for some of his recordings of music at All India Radio Jalandhar. As time passed, Dr Gurnam Singh changed his direction and tilted more and more towards gurmat sangeet, which gave him name and fame in the years that followed.

He started as a lecturer in music at the Punjabi University in Patiala and soon rose to become a highly popular head of department at the university. A few years later he was offered an opportunity to serve the Guru Nanak Dev University in Amritsar as the head of the music department. Since his childhood and formative years were spent in Patiala and Fatehgarh Sahib, he never felt fully at home in the much larger and older city of Amritsar. Hence, when the opportunity again knocked at the door, he went back to Patiala and the Guru Nanak Dev University was left with just a nominal department of musicology. Punjabi University needed a visionary and Dr Gurnam Singh was one. He had a unique quality of getting along very well with the vice chancellors. In fact, he was very close to the brilliant vice chancellor, Swaran Singh Boparai, as well as his successor, Dr Jaspal Singh, an academician of Delhi, who served for three consecutive terms as the vice chancellor of the university. This close relationship was mutually beneficial to both.

One of the advantages of serving in the Punjabi University was the access to some rare gurmat sangeet recordings that had been made in the 1960s and 1970s by stalwarts like Late Bhai Samund Singh and Late Bhai Avtar Singh and Gurcharan Singh. No other university has this kind of library.

During the tenure of Kirpal Singh Narang as the vice chancellor, there was a title of Professor of Guru Granth Sahib Studies and the post was manned by the visionary Dr Taaran Singh (popularly spelt as Taran Singh). He was worried that the old icons of gurmat sangeet were leaving this world one by one. For example, Bhai Santa Singh died in 1966 and Bhai Samund Singh was getting old. He felt that the new generation of Punjabi musicians was not learning music seriously and all that they wanted was to make a quick buck. The concept of riyaz that went on for hours was alien to this generation. All were getting more materialistic and far less spiritual. Hence, he wanted to record as many reets as possible in the highly seasoned voice of Bhai Samund Singh. For this project, he had the full consent of the vice chancellor and money was not an issue. The university arranged a spool type of tape recorder, but it was not the best by any standards. Thus, most of the recording was in mono format.

Bhai Samund Singh was asked to record his life's most precious treasures on this rudimentary electronic gadget. He recorded hundreds of reets which he rendered while being at Gurdwara Janam Asthan at Nankana Sahib and while serving the Golden Temple after 1947. One day a curious Bhai Samund Singh asked Dr Taran Singh the real purpose behind his idea of these elaborate recordings. He explained his apprehension that a day would come when the exponents of these ancient reets would be gone forever and these reets would die with them too. Bhai Samund Singh judged the apprehension and told Dr Taran Singh that some of the most authentic four to five centuries old tunes were still alive within Bhai Jwala Singh's two sons, Bhai Avtar Singh and Bhai Gurcharan Singh. He suggested that this family should also be contacted and recorded.

This led to an invitation sent by the Punjabi University to Bhai Avtar Singh and Gurcharan Singh, who were living in Delhi and were in great demand. Though the money offered to Bhai Samund Singh and Bhai Avtar Singh Gurcharan Singh was a nominal amount but considering a service to the community for its future, both esteemed jathas accepted the proposals.

Bhai Avtar Singh and Gurcharan Singh started recording 500 ancient reets in all 31 raagas of the Sri Guru Granth Sahib sometime around 1970. They would first narrate the wording of the shabad, then identify the raaga and the taal, and then finally begin with the rendition. All along, their tabla master had been their nephew, Bhai Swaran Singh, who learnt to play the tabla from Bhai Jawala Singh and accompanied him for more than five years prior to Bhai Jwala Singh's quitting of shabad kirtan due to old age and failing health.

Bhai Swaran Singh is another important link between Bhai Jawala Singh and his sons and now his grandson, Bhai Kultar Singh, too. He knew all the taals which were used by Bhai Jwala Singh in his kirtan sessions. While quitting shabad kirtan, Bhai Jwala Singh asked his sons to form their own kirtan jatha and persist with the ancient reets that he had taught them as a part of his own jatha. The two brothers, as long as they performed shabad kirtan, persisted with the instructions of their father. They never deviated from the reets that had been taught to them and they never copied Bollywood film tunes.

Bhai Avtar Singh and Gurcharan Singh's recordings included several compositions in the dhrupad style that had been prevalent 500 years ago. Some others were in the dhamar style, a contemporary of the dhrupad.

Partal was a novel idea of rendering each stanza of a Shabad in a different taal. For modern-day kirtanias, all these old practices were completely alien ideas. Bhai Avtar Singh died at the age of 81 and Bhai Gurcharan died at 102! While recording for the university, they made one copy of each reet for themselves too. It turned out to be a very smart idea. They had shared a part of this with me and another part they had shared with Sardar Didar Singh Chana of Toronto, Ontario, Canada. We both have these in our store. Bhai Avtar Singh and Gurcharan Singh wrote the notations of all the reets and recorded it in the book format too. The books were published by the Punjabi University.

These recordings of Bhai Samund Singh and Bhai Avtar Singh and Gurcharan Singh are the initial wealth of the Punjabi University, which is unique to it. No other university or institution anywhere throughout the world has such a rich possession of ancient music.

There is a story that these recordings got damaged due to the extreme heat and humidity of Patiala. There is also a view that someone pilfered these recordings. The truth, though, is that they are all slowly being taken by the Kirtan Sewa Trust of Malaysia who is then publishing them. Some of the gramophone records of pre-1947 icons of Sikh music also have found their way to Malaysia. Wherever possible, the folks at Kirtan Sewa of Malaysia are giving due credit to their lenders of recordings. They are sharing most of these recordings on YouTube also, which gives worldwide exposure to this music.

Dr Gurnam Singh developed the library of Sikh music and created archives of gurmat sangeet with some help though. He has been associated with the Jawaddi Taksal of Sant Sucha Singh in the Ludhiana district. They are great admirers of classical gurmat sangeet and have been holding annual classical kirtan darbars on their campus, where they have been inviting all well-recognised and accomplished kirtanias and recording their music. Dr Gurnam Singh used his good offices with Sant Sucha Singh and later with his equally enthusiastic successors to obtain almost their entire collection of recordings for the archives of Punjabi University. Such things are highly time-consuming, but Gurnam Singh remained adamant.

Dr Gurnam Singh has studied all the raagas of India's leading gharanas as well as gurmat sangeet variations. After finding some free time from his administrative and academic engagements, he has been doing riayz of these raagas. All three brothers make their own tunes and render gurbani in their indigenous compositions. Due to the daily hours of riyaz, Dr Gurnam Singh has developed a highly seasoned and flexible voice now.

According to Madam Santosh Rishi, the Station Director of All India Radio Jalandhar, Dr Gurnam Singh got an 'A' grade after Bhai Bakhshish Singh and Bhai Nirmal Singh Khalsa, but before Bhai Gurmeet Singh Shant. His recordings of shabad kirtan are frequently broadcasted in the Gurbani Vichar Program of All India Radio Jalandhar. He has retired from the Punjabi University and is a freelance academician now, but even after retirement, his demand has not decreased.

Dr Gurnam Singh also popularised Punjab's folk instruments like the king, vanjhali, toombi, toomba, damru (dauru), bughti etc. He went to Sultanpur Lodhi too and visited the village where Bhai Faranda had made a rabab for the use of Bhai Mardana during Guru Nanak Dev ji's udasis. Credit goes to him for rediscovering old string instruments like the taus, saranda and a few others. He got these instruments manufactured and arranged workshops to popularise them as well.

On his recommendation string instruments were introduced in the Golden Temple for accompanying the raagi jathas. While watching the shabad kirtan from the Golden Temple on the TV screens, one can see a fourth man playing a string instrument. Some of them have lately become very proficient in their art. This has been done on Dr Gurnam Singh's insistence.

Some of the books authored or published by him include *Adi Granth Raag Kosh, Punjabi Lok Sangeet Sidhant Sarup, Punjabi Sangeetkar, Sangeet Nibandhavali, Punjabi Bhashayi Shastri Gayan Bandishvali, Gayan Sangeetkar, Gurmat sangeet Prabandh Te Pasar, and Sri Guru Granth Raag Ratnakar.*

Some of the awards conferred on him include the Shiromani Raagi Award by the language department of Punjab in 2001, the fellowship of the Sangeet Natak Academy New Delhi in 2003, the Shiromani Raagi Award by the Punjab Government in 2007, Special Merit Recognition in the art of shabad kirtan by the SGPC in 2008, and the Sangeet Natak Academy of India Award in February of 2019.

Dr Gurnam Singh served on the elite selection committee for hazoori raagis recruited to serve the Golden Temple and the other SGPC-managed historic shrines. The other members used to be Late Bhai Nirmal Singh Khalsa, Professor Kartar Singh, Bhai Ashoke Singh Bagrian, and others. There was a time when scholars of the status of Bhai Vir Singh, Bhai Santa Singh, Bhai Samund Singh, Sardar Jodh Singh of All India Radio, Dilip Chandra Vedi (Dalip Singh Bedi), Giani Chet Singh, and Bhai Aridaman Singh Bagrian of Nabha were consulted to recruit hazoori raagis for the Golden Temple.

In the present-day scenario, though, unfortunately, merit is getting replaced with recommendations. The selection committee is not allowed to exercise its mandated authority.

After retirement, now Dr Gurnam Singh travels a lot. On the personal request of the great philanthropist business tycoon, Sardar Tejinder Singh Bindra, he now serves as a visiting professor at Hofstra University in Long Island, New York. The Guru Nanak Dev University in Amritsar has also requested him to serve as a Professor Emeritus. I suggested to its Vice Chancellor, Dr Jaspal Singh Sandhu, to use the lifelong experience of Dr Gurnam Singh to create a well-meaning library of gurmat sangeet on the lines of the Sikh Musicology Library of the Punjabi University. He has agreed to do that and is awaiting funds from Punjab or the Centre. Let us not forget that Amritsar is the biggest centre of Sikh music, due to the existence of the Golden Temple and the biggest training centre of gurmat sangeet at the Shaheed Sikh Missionary College at Putlighar. Amritsar can use the services of Dr Gurnam Singh a lot better. He has served as a subject expert in the Department of Languages, Punjab, at its head office in Patiala. It goes without saying that Dr Gurnam Singh has been bestowed with the title of Shiromani Kirtania. Given that he is still young and full of energy, his services can be used for years to come.

19

Bhai Gurmeet Singh Shant

A Brilliant Kirtania

Amritsar can be rightly called the nursery of Sikh religious music, thanks primarily to the existence of the Golden Temple, where live music is performed for at least 20 hours every day! People from all over the world visit it every day. In fact, the entire holy area has been blessed by the visits of the Gurus from Amritsar to Khadoor Sahib, Tarn Taran and Goindwal Sahib and has produced hundreds of accomplished musicians in the past.

During the period of the great Gurus, most of the musicians were from the rababi Muslim families hailing from the villages around Amritsar, with only a few exceptions. Bhai Gurmeet Singh Shant's family is one of the practising Sikh families, which took to Sikh religious music as a profession only about five generations ago and now the sixth generation, Bhai Shant's sons, are in it. During his days, Amritsar was saturated with musicians and the competition among them was cutthroat. Yet he carved a niche for himself.

He was born in a family of gursikh classical musicians on 28 February 1966, a few months after the devastating Indo-Pak War of 1965. However, some people believe he was born in 1965. His father's name was Giani Kishan Singh Shant, who had been a trained Sikh religious musician popular in the Amritsar area. His grandfather, Sant Surain Singh, and his great grandfather, Baba Charan Dass, were both popular exponents of Sikh religious music. They all lived in their ancestral village of Muchhal which was merely a kilometre off the Amritsar-Delhi Grand Trunk Road near Jandiala Guru. He had been introduced to gurbani and gurmat sangeet from a very young age by his father who wanted to see his favourite son as a leading Sikh religious musician. He started his formal education in the village primary school.

In his childhood, he was exposed to the performances of Punjab's leading classical musicians performing music at the Radio Pakistan in Lahore, which, during those days, was the most powerful radio station and was the most heard one too. Pakistan's finest musicians took pleasure in performing at this station. Among its leading artists were Nazaqat Ali Khan, Salamat Ali Khan who formerly belonged to Sham Churasi in Hoshiarpur, Amanat Ali Khan, Fateh Ali Khan, Tufail Niazi of Kapurthala, Farida Khanum of Amritsar, Mallika Pukhraj of Jammu and Zahida Perveen of Amritsar. Not only did he learn from his ustad, but also by intensively listening to the recordings and live radio performances of great masters.

Bhai Gurmeet Singh Shant in the middle

When Amritsar was badly battered by the Indo-Pak war in 1965, his father decided to move the family to some other place. That is how they reached New Delhi in 1970, where his father received the job of a priest-cum-raagi in a neighbourhood gurdwara. The stay of any rural person in a larger city is always an education in itself. His father learnt a lot of refinement from his stay in the national capital. In the meanwhile, he kept coaching young Gurmeet Singh Shant during which time his elder brothers became full-fledged kirtanias. They stayed for seven years, up to 1977, in Delhi. There was a clear indication that as Delhi was getting modernised, it became more and more of a cosmopolitan city. In other words, Delhi was fast losing its character as a city of Punjabis displaced from Pakistan. The Shant family did not want to lose their typical Punjabi character and wanted to return to a place where the Punjabi language and culture was still thriving.

Their decision to return to Punjab was finalised. From 1977 to 1979, they stayed in their ancestral village, Muchhal after which the family moved to Jalandhar. This city had the added advantage of being the home to Punjab's capital radio station. It had some brilliant trainers and accomplished musical instrument players associated with the broadcasting industry.

Bhai Sahib passed his matriculation examination from Jalandhar in 1981. Even during his school days, he cultivated the instinct to compete and excel in music. In pursuance of his lofty goal, he took an active part in music and gurbani recital competitions, wherever those were held, and won several prizes due to his grit and determination to excel. He was quite athletically built, and he won some prizes as a football player in Jalandhar too. He claims to be a good cricketer as well.

Being an ace footballer, he had to build up good running speed and stamina. However, his primary objective in life was to become a leading Sikh religious musician at the Jalandhar station of All India Radio and to achieve the status of a well-respected hazoori raagi at the Golden Temple in Amritsar. He pursued both aims with perfect professional dedication.

His first exposure to competitive gurmat sangeet was at the Lyallpur Khalsa Higher Secondary School in Jalandhar for participation in the Martyrdom Day of Guru Teg Bahadur ji commemorations on the 12 December 1980. Before that, he had won second prize in the kirtan competition at Sri Guru Arjan Dev Khalsa Higher Secondary School in Tarn Taran in 1980. He got a certificate of merit from the Service Training Centre in Jalandhar for performing bhakti sangeet during a competition on 17 October 1981. Bhai Gurmeet Singh Shant also won the coveted Best Performance Award given by the Ashram of Swami Mohan Dass in 1982. He won the second prize at a kirtan competition at the Guru Gobind Singh Study Circle held on 6 March 1982. He won a merit certificate from Lyallpur Khalsa Higher Secondary School again in 1983 on the Martyrdom Day of Guru Teg Bahadur ji. He participated in the shabad kirtan competition at Ramgarhia Higher Secondary School in the neighbouring town of Phagwara too.

He took a course – Junior Diploma (Vocal) – from the Prayag Sangeet Samiti of Allahabad in Uttar Pradesh in 1982 and passed the examination with first division. He completed his Giani Course from Panjab University in 1988. Additionally, he passed the Sangeet Visharad (Vocal) from the Pracheen Kala Kendra in Chandigarh in 1986-1987, again, by scoring a first division grade.

Before attaining the age of 20, Bhai Gurmeet Singh Shant had learnt so much gurbani by heart and had practised so many raagas that he had no difficulty in forming his own well-meaning raagi jatha. His brothers, Kuldip Singh and Manjit Singh, completed the trio. Kuldip Singh played the harmonium and Manjit Singh accompanied him on the tabla. This group was formed in 1985. Within a short span of time, his group became popular not only in the city of Jalandhar but also in the rest of Bist Doab. Those who liked classical music preferred his jatha. He was engaged to perform gurmat sangeet on both happy and sad occasions at several places in Kapurthala, Phagwara and Hoshiarpur, as well as at Ludhiana and Amritsar.

As a lifelong student of music, Bhai Gurmeet Singh Shant has a firm belief that once you have the necessary command over the raagas, music can also be learnt by repeatedly listening to the performances of great masters of the past and singing along with their recordings. In pursuance of this aim, he mastered some of the difficult musical compositions of Late Bhai Samund Singh through his dilruba accompaniment Bhai Chattar Singh of All India Radio. He has repeatedly listened to some of the choicest compositions of Late Bhai Bakhshish Singh and Late Bhai Balbir Singh. After mastering the compositions of great masters, he started singing those compositions often. I don't mind listening to his repeat renditions. He has learnt some of the greatest musical compositions of Late Bhai Santa Singh too, which he claims that at the time of my writing about him, he had not recorded. However, he did express his inclination to record them. Having the knowledge of all 31 raagas of the Sri Guru Granth Sahib, he performs shabad kirtan in the prescribed raagas. Very few people have this unique ability.

After becoming a jathedar and picking up more confidence, he started performing shabad kirtan at far off places outside Punjab too. On many occasions, he undertook a tour of Chandigarh, Patiala. Mohali and several cities in Haryana. Many times, due to compulsions of circumstances, his other two members of the jatha kept changing. One of his relatives, and a brilliant student, is Bhai Karamjit Singh Shant who now lives in New York. His voice is very melodious. Sometimes he accompanies Bhai Gurmeet Singh Shant. He is the owner of a taxicab, but in his spare time, he performs shabad kirtan in the gurdwaras of New York, New Jersey, Connecticut and Boston.

In 1992, Bhai Gurmeet Singh Shant appeared for an audition test in front of a panel of expert judges of music at All India Radio Jalandhar. He passed the test and was offered a general grade. After that, he started regular singing at the radio station. His voice became even more popular and that increased his overall demand. Since the medium-wave service of All India Radio Jalandhar is heard even beyond New Delhi, his demand took a quantum jump beyond the boundaries of Punjab too. Demand for his kirtan came from Delhi, Uttarakhand and Uttar Pradesh. On special occasions, he even went as far away as Sri Huzoor Sahib in Nanded, Maharashtra and Takhat Sri Patna Sahib in Bihar. The knowledgeable sangat of Mumbai invites him often on special occasions.

Giani Sant Singh Maskeen was a great lover of gurmat sangeet, and he was particularly fond of the shabad kirtan skills of Bhai Gurmeet Singh Shant. This, he specially performed at his place in Alwar (Rajasthan).

Maskeen ji, in fact, often took him on his tours to different parts of India.

Late Sant Sucha Singh of Jawaddi in Ludhiana was a great promoter of classical gurmat sangeet. He used to hold an annual gurmat sangeet sammelan in his taksal. Since the 1990s, Bhai Gurmeet Singh Shant and party have been regular participants in it. On different occasions he has taken part in all the chowkis and performed kirtan in the prescribed raagas in accordance with time. His talent has been publicly acknowledged by Sant Sucha Singh and his successors.

On the birth anniversary of Sri Guru Ram Das ji, normally held in the month of October, a kirtan darbar in raagas is held every year at the Manji Sahib Diwan Hall of the Golden Temple. It is a great honour to be invited to perform in it. Bhai Gurmeet Singh Shant has been invited to it every year also since the 1990s. In addition to being a versatile vocalist, he is considered an accomplished harmonium and tabla player too. In the art of tabla playing, he understands most of the taals used by the kirtanias. The other instruments that he plays proficiently include the taus and the surmandal. He is a quick learner and grasps difficult tunes effortlessly.

The largest Sikh population outside India lives in the United Kingdom. Since the Doaba region of Punjab is known for its diaspora, more demand for his visits to the United Kingdom, the United States of America and Canada arose. From time to time, he visited all these countries. He had a highly successful tour of Canada in 2000 and 2001. His American visit, especially to the New York and New Jersey areas, in 2001, was very hectic and successful. His visits to England have been more frequent in 1997–99 and again in 2001 and 2003.

He was specially invited to perform shabad kirtan at the *dera* of Sant Sujan Singh in New Delhi. The sangat in this dera consisted primarily of refugees from Peshawar, Rawalpindi and Multan divisions. They liked his style of kirtan so much that they gave him a gold medal. In 1999, All India Radio Jalandhar elevated him to a high B-grade. The Mata Kaulan Bhalai Kendra in Amritsar, located very close to the Golden Temple, also invited him to perform several chowkis of shabad kirtan and awarded him a gold medal.

All India Radio Jalandhar, after observing his dedication and responsibility to duty, in 2006, elevated him to A-grade. They felt that he was the most deserving candidate in the category of shabad kirtan. Bhai Nirmal Singh was the only other male A-class kirtania of All India Radio who passed away on 2 April 2020. Now the folks at All India Radio Jalandhar are left with only one male A-class artist in the category of Sikh devotional music. When he is not on a tour abroad, he is readily available for every big occasion at this radio station.

A long-time president of the Shiromani Gurdwara Prabandhak Committee Amritsar, Jathedar Avtar Singh Makkar, was extremely fond of Bhai Gurmeet Singh Shant's gurmat sangeet skills. He very well knew the shortage of good musicians in the SGPC. His desire was to recruit at least one highly skilled kirtania in the service of Sri Darbar Sahib. In 2012, he invited Bhai Gurmeet Singh Shant to become a hazoori raagi of the Golden Temple. This coveted duty he performed with distinction for seven years up to 2018. During this tenure, he performed kirtan in all the chowkis starting from 'Asa Di Vaar' up to the *sukhasan*[70] time. He performed shabad kirtan in all 31 raagas in accordance with the time of the raaga. This is a rare quality in musicians.

During one of the celebrations of the Martyrdom Day of Sri Guru Teg Bahadur ji at Gurdwara Sis Ganj Sahib in Old Delhi, a three-day long special kirtan *samagam*[71] was held. Bhai Harjit Singh and Bhai Gurdip Singh were entrusted with the responsibilities of stage secretary. In this samagam, Bhai Gurmeet Singh Shant was especially honoured as a highly accomplished

---

[70] When performed at the end of the normal Gurdwara day, it is normally a ritual or ceremonial declaration to mark the fact that the Guru's court having closed for the day. Guru Granth Sahib retires to the special bed which is normally housed in a different location from the Darbar Hall.

[71] Religious gathering.

kirtania of the Sikh *jagat*.[72] He gets frequent invitations to perform shabad kirtan in Delhi's historic gurdwaras.

His shabad kirtan in all the raagas is preserved in the form of video and audio formats. PTC has exclusive rights to all the transcripts and recordings in the Golden Temple. Some of his best recordings in the sanctum sanctorum of the Golden Temple are also available on YouTube. He was extensively recorded on CDs and DVDs by reputed companies like T-Series, Frankfin, Amrit Bani, Shemaroo, Red Records Amritsar, and Fine Touch Amritsar (30 CDs).

During all the big celebrations, he was invited to perform prime time shabad kirtan either at the government-sponsored programs or at the sponsored programs of SGPC, DSGMC, Patna Sahib, Huzoor Sahib or the other organisations. During the 550th birth anniversary of Guru Nanak Dev ji held in Sultanpur Lodhi, he was the main performer of shabad kirtan. Similarly, on the 400th birth anniversary celebration at the home of the then Tourism and Culture Minister, Mr Charanjit Singh Channi, he was the leading kirtania. On the birth anniversary of Guru Gobind Singh ji he performed the special

[72] world

shabad kirtan at the Takhat Sri Patna Sahib in 2021. His present raagi jatha consists of his son, Bhai Padampreet Singh, and Kuldip Singh. He is one of the best kirtanias today.

20

A One-of-a-Kind Kirtan Darbar

During the late 1950s or early 1960s, a few lovers of gurmat sangeet in Delhi put their heads together to plan a unique kirtan darbar in which only the most technically sound Sikh religious musicians would participate. After a protracted debate, they zeroed in on only four musicians. One of the invited musicians was Bhai Santa Singh, the leading musician at the Gurdwara Sri Sis Ganj Sahib in Old Delhi. The second one was Bhai Samund Singh of Ludhiana (formerly of Gurdwara Janam Asthan Sri Nankana Sahib and the Golden Temple Amritsar). The third invited jatha consisted of Bhai Avtar Singh and Gurcharan Singh – hazoori raagis of Gurdwara Sri Sis Ganj Sahib. The fourth invitee was Sant Sujan Singh of Karol Bagh and Rajouri Garden (formerly of Lyallpur in West Punjab).

Normally the kirtan darbars are held in the evenings or after 8 a.m., but this one started in the fourth pehar of the night, or after 3 a.m. The rendition of 'Asa Di Vaar' was split into two parts – the first part of 12 chhakkas and some other shabads was to be rendered by Bhai Santa Singh and his jatha and the second half, consisting of the remaining 12 chhakkas of 'Asa Di Vaar' and some other shabads, was to be rendered by Bhai Avtar Singh Gurcharan Singh. The time allotted to both jathas was one hour each.

The next segment consisted of one hour of shabad kirtan performed by Sant Sujan Singh. This was followed by two short segments of 30 minutes each by Bhai Avtar Singh Gurcharan Singh and by Bhai Santa Singh and his jatha. The last segment, which was to last for more than an hour was allotted to Bhai Samund Singh and he finished the program with six pauris of Anand Sahib.

By nearly 10 a.m., the program was over. While eating breakfast, the musicians exchanged their views. Bhai Samund Singh was the most vocal. He told Sant Sujan Singh that his voice was very sweet. He asked Sant ji if he had trained any shagird because he feared that Sant Sujan Singh's melodious style in qawwali ang will die if no one continues it after him. Sant Sujan Singh replied that his son, Surjit Singh, was his shagird and he would continue the tradition.

Bhai Samund Singh was of the opinion that all the reets that he heard from Bhai Santa Singh were derived from Sikh classical music, but the camouflaging was so perfect that to a layman, it appeared non-classical. Everybody else agreed that Bhai Santa Singh was a great exponent of the Guru's baani and that during his high notes he talked directly to the Guru!

About Bhai Avtar Singh Gurcharan Singh, everybody was unanimous that if dhrupad and dhamar were still alive in Sikh music and compositions of partal exist to this day, it is because of the meticulous training imparted by Bhai Jawala Singh to his sons, who are continuing his legacy when most others have switched to the khayali format of classical music.

Everybody agreed that Bhai Samund Singh, due to his uninterrupted long durations of riyaz, had trained his voice remarkably well and that he could render every difficult nuance of the shabad kirtan with utmost ease. Every raagi jatha thought that Bhai Samund Singh even talked in terms of classical music. In age, too, Bhai Samund Singh was the oldest.

This story was narrated to me by none other than Giani Gurdip Singh, the then head priest of Sikh Cultural Society Gurdwara at 118th Street in Richmond Hill Area of the Queens Borough of New York City. He was a great and knowledgeable lover of gurmat sangeet. During his tenure as the head priest at the Gurdwara Richmond Hill, India's finest Sikh musicians were invited to America. His son, Nachhattar Singh, is also a great lover of gurmat sangeet. Giani Gurdip Singh was deeply worried at the plummeting standard of music at the Golden Temple, which at one time was the torchbearer of gurmat sangeet in the entire world.

21

All India Radio and Sikh Music

Sikh religious music was judged by the same yardstick as any other music at Punjab's oldest radio station, All India Radio Lahore. Lahore had the advantage of two popular places of Sikh religious music, the Golden Temple in Amritsar and the Gurdwara Janam Asthan Sri Nankana Sahib in its close vicinity. The Golden Temple was 36 miles to the east of Lahore and Nankana Sahib was 50 miles away to the southwest of Lahore. In addition, the Gurdwara Dera Sahib in Lahore hosted several good musicians from time to time.

In 1937, the year of its inception, All India Radio Lahore approved two musicians, one each from the Golden Temple and Nankana Sahib. The one from the Golden Temple was Bhai Santa Singh, a specialist in applied classical music and from Nankana Sahib it was Bhai Samund Singh, an exponent of pure classical music, in the Sikh terminology called gurmat sangeet. Both rose to become A-class artists of All India Radio Delhi and Jalandhar respectively. In addition, several others were approved, including Bhai Piara Singh and some musicians of Nankana Sahib.

At that time All India Radio was exercising a lot of restraints on its musicians. The musicians had to finish their pieces with a set time limit. For example, the item had to be completed within four-and-a-half minutes, seven minutes, and nine-and-a-half minutes. In reality, the half-minute was reserved for announcements. In the case of Bhai Samund Singh, the longest pieces lasted close to 15-20 minutes. Bhai Santa Singh mostly recorded for shorter durations. He avoided the repetition of stanzas as far as possible. Sikh music was awarded as much time as naats and qawwalis at All India Radio Lahore.

After the creation of Pakistan, most of the naat singers crossed over from the Indian Punjab into Pakistan and the Sikh religious musicians crossed over to India. When radio opened its doors in Indian Punjab, many more musicians were approved. This included Bhai Amrik Singh of Amritsar, Bhai Avtar Singh Gurcharan Singh of Sultanpur Lodhi, Bhai Munsha Singh of Kapurthala, and Bhai Harchand Singh of Ludhiana. Later, Bhai Davinder Singh of Gurdaspur and Bhai Bakhshish Singh of Patiala were also approved. All were made to pass through vigorous time constraints though. At the radio stations, only the formally approved musicians were allowed to perform, and everyone was paid according to his/her classification.

I have heard stories of how All India Radio Lahore, or for that matter Radio Pakistan, Lahore, chased the talent, brought the would-be artists to the station and approved them as radio artists. However, the same kind of spirit had been missing at All India Radio Jalandhar. Many musicians of great calibre like Bhai Didar Singh of village Nangal Khurd district Hoshiarpur, Bhai Pal Singh and Bhai Jaswant Singh of Nankana Sahib, Bhai Gurmukh Singh Sarmukh Singh Fakkar of Nankana Sahib, Bhai Prithipal Singh Mohan Pal Singh of Patiala, Bhai Joginder Singh Mohinder Singh of Patiala, Bhai Jagtar Singh Fakkar of Patiala, Bhai Harinder Singh Harcharan Singh Fakkar of Patiala, and Bhai Beant Singh Bijli of Phillaur are just a few names who were ignored.

Moreover, when the 78-RPM records were replaced, the entirety of the music available on those records could not be converted into long-playing and extended play records or radio station tapes. Similarly, when the long-playing records were abandoned, for all the musicians, the backup tapes were not made and when the taped music was transferred onto the compact discs and pen drives, the music on discarded systems was never fully transferred onto the adopted systems. This is how a lot of music of the iconic musicians got wasted. Such a loss is not a temporary loss, it is an irreparable loss for posterity.

On the contrary, Sri Lanka Broadcasting Corporation (SLBC) in Colombo, Sri Lanka, popularly known as Radio Ceylon, has kept its entire collection of 78-RPM records, 45-RPM records and 33.33-RPM long-playing records permanently preserved in its fully secured storage vaults. They keep playing this music regularly in their shortwave service on 11,905 kHz in the mornings.

I have seen all kinds of record-playing, cassette-playing and compact-disc-recording-and-playing-systems at work in the scores of studios at the Voice of America Head Office in Washington D.C. I believe All India Radio needs to learn a lot from the Voice of America, BBC in London and SLBC in Colombo. I am not very sure about Radio Pakistan though. At one time they had a lot of old recordings, but I am unsure of the status currently.

Some recorded Sikh religious music at various stations of All India Radio can still be traced if a concerted effort is made. Some private collectors do have some of the old recordings, perhaps of All India Radio Delhi and Jalandhar in their possession. Some have shared their collections with the Kirtan Sewa Society of Malaysia and Gurmat Sangeet Project of Boston, Massachusetts, USA. In return, the Kirtan Sewa Society of Malaysia has shared most of their music on YouTube and the Gurmat Sangeet Project of Sarbpreet Singh has shared it through its archives. More such music deserves to be discovered and saved. Also, attempts should be made to broadcast it over All India Radio by discarding antiquated rules of paying royalty.

The Central Sikh Museum at the Golden Temple and the Sikh Reference Library, also at the Golden Temple should approach the Kirtan Sewa Society of Malaysia, the Gurmat Sangeet Project of Boston in the USA, and the Panjabi University of Patiala to share their unique collections of gurmat sangeet for preservation at a central place. A time will come when researchers shall like to sift through these treasures to fulfil their research dreams.

Some collectors like Sital Singh Shownki of Amritsar and Mandeep Singh Sidhu of Patiala, are collecting old music. I shall appeal to them to collect old records of gurmat sangeet also. Sital Singh Shownki does have several old records of rare kirtanias. I have told him to preserve it for future generations and he has paid attention to my request.

22

Dehradun is Developing as a New Centre of Sikh Music

Impressed by his teachings, more than 500 years ago, during Sri Guru Nanak Dev ji's udasi, a lot of local people from the areas constituting the present states of Uttar Pradesh and Uttarakhand became his followers. Some of them are now fully practising amritdhari Sikhs. Some of them have become pracharaks, while others have learnt gurmat sangeet and are now raagis at numerous gurdwaras in India and abroad. One of their most-reputed and highly motivated teachers was Giani Dayal Singh, who first learnt the Sikh religious music himself from the finest experts and then started teaching gurmat sangeet to his pupils. He shifted his base to Gurdwara Sri Raqab Ganj Sahib in New Delhi, from where he produced a lot of highly accomplished Sikh religious musicians. He adopted a highly disciplinarian regime.

Some of Bhai Dayal Singh's most brilliant students include Bhai Surjit Singh, who now lives in Long Island New York in the USA. Bhai Surjit Singh had properly learnt the Dhrupad and Dhamar style of music from Giani Dyal Singh. He can proficiently sing partals as well as *guldastas*.[73] Of

---

[73] *Guldasta* is the rendition of same *shabad* by changing the *alaap* from one basic *raaga* to several others.

course, he can also sing a complete khayal from alaap to jorh alaap, vilambit, madh lai, and dhrutt. He is adept at choosing rare taals for his renditions. He is a very quiet person but highly accomplished and quite a popular musician in America. In India, though, hardly anyone in the SGPC knows about him.

Another great musician of Dehradun is Bhai Kanwar Pal Singh. He is also a brilliant musician of gurmat sangeet with a good voice and has done a lot of riyaz of the classical raagas. He also knows almost every raaga that Bhai Surjit Singh of Long Island of New York knows. He is one of the favourites of the Late Giani Dayal Singh. Some of his recordings are available on YouTube.

Another versatile musician of Dehradun is Bhai Prakash Singh (some spell it as Parkash Singh). He came to Gurdwara Bridgewater in New Jersey during the 1990s. He was introduced to me by Dr Gurparkash Singh, a scientist in the pharmacy industry in America. At that time, I was involved in the management of Gurdwara Bridgewater, Somerset County, New Jersey in the USA. I found Prakash Singh to be a quick learner and a very patient teacher of gurmat sangeet. To me, he was suitable as a permanent musician in the gurdwara. He was also willing to teach gurmat sangeet to the school-going children. Being a native of Uttar Pradesh, his Punjabi was not very good, but he could more than compensate for this weakness of his with his very helpful attitude and polite manner. On his own, he started teaching raagas vocally and started teaching the art of playing the harmonium as an instrument. His companion singer, Bhai Shivcharan Singh, also did the same as did his tabla player and companion, Bhai Harbhajan Singh.

Another raagi from Uttar Pradesh, Bhai Vinod Singh, who learnt the art of tabla playing from a famous musical gharana of Benares, also started teaching the art of tabla playing to the school students who attended the gurdwara's Sunday school. Over the years, this group from Uttar Pradesh became an asset for the gurdwara. Added to this, every week they enthralled the audience with one or two unheard-of reets.

I had a huge collection of vintage gurmat sangeet with me. I shared one reet at a time with Bhai Parkash Singh. He used to practice it at home for a whole week and on the following Sunday, he used to sing it before the congregation. After a few years of uninterrupted service at just one particular gurdwara, some members of the sangat wanted a change. The change did happen. Later, however, when the raagi jatha decided to move on to a new gurdwara, some people repented after their decision. Bhai Parkash Singh's group moved to the newly established Sikh Sangat of Central New Jersey Gurdwara in the Lawrenceville area of Mercer County in New Jersey. Here, they now perform kirtan duty and teach gurmat sangeet. Bhai Parkash Singh has a shrill voice, which can be used for proficiently singing some of the most difficult compositions of Late Bhai Santa Singh ji too. He still has a long way to go though as he is still learning music. I am eager to listen to him again.

Another highly accomplished pupil of Giani Dayal Singh is now serving as a hazoori raagi at the Golden Temple in Amritsar. His name is Bhai Rai Singh. Today he is counted among the most respected musicians of the Golden Temple.

Bhai Dayal Singh is no more, but the fragrance of the students he trained will be felt as long as his pupils are alive in India and abroad.

23

Sarbpreet Singh and the Gurmat Sangeet Project

Sarbpreet Singh hails from a well-to-do Sikh family of contractors in Punjab and Assam, which have commercial interests in several northeastern Indian states. He is an engineer by profession, but within him, he always had the seed of a lover of Sikh religious music that was waiting to germinate. Young Sarbpreet Singh always admired the music of good Sikh religious musicians of the yesteryears. I found him admiring the art of Bhai Avtar Singh and Gurcharan Singh, Bhai Shamsher Singh Zakhmi and Bhai Mohan Pal Singh, and Bhai Didar Singh.

I saw him first in New Jersey during the mid-1980s. He was seen in the weekly congregation in Gurdwara Bridgewater, Somerset County, New Jersey. He is related to the famous Gurbakhsh Singh Preetlari, a legendry Sikh social writer and the founder of an artists' colony known as Preet Nagar in rural Amritsar.

He always had the option of going to Gurdwara Glenrock New Jersey too, but he liked to visit Gurdwara Bridgewater.

One of his good friends is Dr Gurparkash Singh, a scientist associated with the pharmacy industry.

When he began learning gurmat sangeet, occasionally, he would request the management to give him a chance to render shabads in the gurdwara. Soon he started collecting recordings of gurmat sangeet of Bhai Samund Singh and Bhai Santa Singh. I gave him some music too which I had collected over the years. Dr Gurparkash Singh, S. Manjeet Singh Deoorey, and S. Manjit Singh of Amritsar always encouraged him in his endeavour at Gurdwara Bridgewater. At one time, we all wanted him to be a part of the management of the gurdwara, but he was unwilling to take on any such assignment. Against his wishes, he was appointed as the secretary of the working committee. However, Sarbpreet Singh was the odd man out in the committee. Ultimately, the arrangement did not work, but we discovered a brilliant stage secretary in him.

Sarbpreet Singh has been very good with computer technology. He intended to preserve the finest Sikh religious music on an exclusive website. So, he created a website named www.gurmatsangeetproject.com. On this website, he put some rare recordings of the gurmat sangeet.

When he moved to Boston, he started promoting good Sikh musicians over there. He developed a special liking for Giani Dayal Singh, a brilliant teacher of Sikh music from Uttar Pradesh who had settled in New Delhi, where he taught vintage Sikh religious music to a lot of students from the state and even elsewhere in India. Some of his trainees who settled in the USA include Bhai Surjit Singh of Long Island and Bhai Prakash Singh of the Sikh Sabha Gurdwara of Central Jersey in Lawrence Township of Mercer County. Another great musician is Bhai Kanwar Pal Singh of Dehradun, who shuttles between India and the USA. One other pupil of his, Bhai Rai Singh is a musician in the SGPC. He performs his duties at the Golden Temple in Amritsar.

Sarbpreet Singh also arranges special kirtan darbars at various gurdwaras in the USA. He also arranges simulcasts of these kirtan darbars, and has prepared special folders on the Late Bhai Santa Singh, Late Bhai Samund Singh, Late Bhai Dharam Singh Zakhmi, Late Bhai Gian Singh Almast, Bhai Thakar Singh, Late Bhai Shamsher Singh Zakhmi, Late Bhai Didar Singh, and so many others. He is the kind of person who does not mind spending lots of dollars from his own pocket for preserving gurmat sangeet. I am truly impressed by his dedication and commitment to gurmat sangeet.